Conversations with Greg Laurie and Chuck Swindoll

Passion *for the* Gospel

Practical Help on How to Share Your Faith

PASSION FOR THE GOSPEL

From the Bible-Teaching Ministries of
Charles R. Swindoll and Greg Laurie

Published by IFL Publishing House, A Division of Insight for Living
Post Office Box 251007, Plano, Texas 75025-1007

Editor in Chief: Cynthia Swindoll, President, Insight for Living
Executive Vice President: Wayne Stiles, Th.M., D.Min., Dallas Theological Seminary
Editor: Brie Engeler, B.A., University Scholars, Baylor University
Copy Editor: Jim Craft, M.A., English, Mississippi College
Proofreaders: Melissa Carlisle, M.A., Christian Education, Dallas Theological Seminary
      Mike Penn, B.A., Journalism, University of Oklahoma
Cover Designer: Steven Tomlin, Embry-Riddle Aeronautical University, 1992–1995
Production Artist: Nancy Gustine, B.F.A., Advertising Art, University of North Texas
Cover Photo: JupiterImages
      Photo of Chuck Swindoll courtesy of Phil Bruce
      Photo of Greg Laurie courtesy of Trinity Broadcasting Network

ISBN 978-1-57972-722-2
Printed in the United States of America

Table of Contents

Introduction from Chuck and Greg

Most of us are reluctant to witness for Jesus Christ for several reasons. One is our feeling of ignorance. We don't really know how to go about it. Another is our fear of a hostile response. So we don't risk it.

But the basic feeling among many Christians is, *I'll leave evangelism for the professional. I'll let the preacher do it, and I'll just pick up the tab.* And we shift that responsibility to someone else—maybe to an evangelist at a crusade, like Greg Laurie, where he, so gifted, is able to declare Christ so well.

But sharing Christ is not just a gift . . . it's a command. And a marvelous privilege.

Nobody likes to be evangelized, but *everybody likes good news!* My hope is that this resource that Greg and I have contributed to will help you put the "good news" back in the gospel.

That's our passion.

Chuck Swindoll

—Charles R. Swindoll

Chuck Swindoll is a real treasure in the church today. He is one of the most gifted communicators, hands down—whether through preaching or writing—that I have ever heard or read. I have been taught and deeply touched through his words time and time again.

It has been a real privilege for me to co-labor with Chuck in this new resource on the timely topic of evangelism. We are both engaged in the serious work of ministry, but I must say, we had a lot of fun working on this project together.

I hope that you can catch our shared passion to obey the Lord's marching orders to "Go into all the world and preach the gospel."

—Greg Laurie

Charles R. Swindoll

Accuracy, clarity, and practicality all describe the Bible-teaching ministry of Dr. Charles R. Swindoll. Chuck is the chairman of the board of Insight for Living and the chancellor of Dallas Theological Seminary. He also serves as the senior pastor of Stonebriar Community Church in Frisco, Texas, where he is able to do what he loves most—teach the Bible to willing hearts.

Chuck's congregation extends far beyond a local church body. Since 1979, he has served as the Bible teacher on *Insight for Living*. Chuck's sermons are broadcast in every major Christian radio market in all fifty states, through more than two thousand outlets worldwide, in numerous foreign languages, and to a growing Webcast audience.

Contributing more than sixty-five titles to an international reading audience, Chuck's extensive writing ministry has been recognized by the Evangelical Press Association. He has also received twelve Gold Medallion awards. His most influential books include *Strengthening Your Grip*, *Laugh Again*, *The Grace Awakening*, and the *Great Lives from God's Word* series.

Chuck Swindoll enjoys life and laughter and finds pleasure in exploring God's Word as well as His world. Those who know Chuck best appreciate his commitment to Jesus Christ, to his family, and to his role as shepherd-teacher. Chuck and Cynthia, his wife of more than fifty years, have four grown children and ten grandchildren. They reside in Frisco, Texas.

Greg Laurie

*G*reg Laurie pastors Harvest Christian Fellowship (one of America's largest churches) in Riverside, California. He has authored several books including the Gold Medallion Award winner, *The Upside-Down Church*, as well as *Losers and Winners*, *Saints and Sinners*, and *The Best Is Yet to Come*. You can find his study notes in the *New Believer's Bible* and *The Seeker's Bible*.

Host of the *Harvest: Greg Laurie* television program and the nationally syndicated radio program *A New Beginning*, he is also the founder and featured speaker for Harvest Crusades—contemporary, large-scale, evangelistic outreaches, which local churches organize nationally and internationally. Greg has also appeared on CNN's *Larry King Live*, *ABC World News Tonight*, *Fox News*, and *MSNBC*, sharing how the Bible is relevant for people today.

Whether speaking or writing, God has gifted Greg with the ability to apply biblical principles to current events in a way that is relevant and easily understood by people of all ages, from all walks of life. The trademark of a Greg Laurie sermon, book, or broadcast is his contemporary, yet straightforward style and format. He resides in Southern California with his wife, Cathe.

Passion *for* *the* Gospel

Chapter 1

A Conversation between Chuck and Greg

Recently, Chuck Swindoll and Greg Laurie met in the recording studio to discuss one of the most important subjects in the Bible. An ideal conversation between the preacher and the evangelist is that of sharing the good news with those who don't know Jesus Christ—Chuck and Greg obliged.

Dave Spiker, the announcer for both Insight for Living *and* A New Beginning *broadcasts, began the conversation on a lighthearted note.*

❧

Dave: Now, Chuck and Greg, our listeners know you both have a passion for God's Word. You both have a passion for reaching the unsaved. But they may not know that you share another passion. You both have a love for a particular mode of transportation. . . . [*Plays audio of Harley-Davidson motorcycles.*]

Chuck: Oh, yes, yes. That's the sound of heaven right there!

Dave: You guys not only ride Harleys, but you've actually ridden together before. Is that right?

Chuck and Greg: Oh, yeah.

Dave: And I know that, well, Greg, it seems to me I've heard that after riding with Chuck Swindoll, you had a souvenir.

Chuck: Careful, careful, Greg . . . be careful where you go with this.

Greg: Well, we did go out on a ride a number of years ago, and I was very excited to go riding with Chuck on our Harleys. And we're out riding, and we have a mutual friend named David that was with us as well. And we're not out on the road like two minutes, and I get pulled over by the CHP on a freeway.

Chuck: That . . . that represents a policeman. CHP. I want to make sure folks know that, Greg.

Greg: California Highway Patrol. And so I was pulled over and . . . and I . . . I guess I was exceeding the speed limit.

Chuck: I guess!

Greg: So David and Chuck pulled over up the road, and they tried to come back. And this officer—he was kind of like Barney Fife or something—he said, "Get back on your motorcycles and move on." And so they said, "Okay," and they rode off. And I just thought, *I can't believe this is happening to me. Why does it have to be the one time I go riding with Chuck that I get a ticket?* It was humiliating. Kind of funny too. And, of course, I used it in a sermon.

Dave: Everything's fair if it's for a sermon illustration. Well, we probably should do some proper introductions. Greg Laurie is the senior pastor of Harvest Christian Fellowship in Riverside, California. He's the author of a number of books and the speaker for Harvest Crusades, and of course, the Bible-teacher each day on *A New Beginning*. And Pastor Chuck Swindoll is senior pastor of Stonebriar Community Church in Frisco, Texas. He's the author of dozens of books and also chancellor of Dallas Theological Seminary. And, of course, he's the daily

Bible-teacher on *Insight for Living*. Chuck, I know you've visited Greg's evangelistic Harvest Crusade.

Chuck: Yes, I have.

Dave: These Harvest Crusades have reached out to over three million people. More than a quarter of a million have registered decisions for Christ. And I know you attended, Chuck.

Chuck: Well, I have. He invites sinners, so I was invited, you know. I remember sitting on the platform one time and thinking, *You know, my kids need to be a part of this; they need to see this in action.* I brought one of our sons, and he was right up there with me. I said, "You need to watch this. Now, listen to this message." And he did. And, of course, he's heard me all his life. But he heard a very gifted evangelist that day as Greg shared the good news. He had a way of wrapping it around a wonderful story that he told. And boy, my son was just on the edge of his seat. And then I said, "Now watch; watch God work." And we've all seen this at the Graham Crusade. We think, *I've heard all this before, and people aren't going to be that responsive.* And they just climbed over seats to get down front! I guess you'll never get over the thrill of that, Greg.

Greg: It never gets old to me. And it's a huge, big leap of faith, you know, when you invite people to come to Christ. If you believe that God's Word is true, you must believe there's authority in it. But there's always that moment of pause where people are deciding what they're going to do, and you're just trusting in God. I have to say, during that moment, it's a time of great spiritual warfare for the preacher, as you know, Chuck, when you give invitations.

I asked Billy Graham once, "What do you feel, what are you experiencing when you give an invitation?" His response was, "I feel like power is going out of me." I think he was talking about that conflict, that friction, that pressure that's happening as people are making the decision for time and eternity.

Chuck: Well, I think it's the unseen world which is far more real than the seen. And we, at that moment, tap into that realm of battle. The battle for souls is a deep and constant thing—especially for people whose lives have never been impacted with the truth. They've walked in darkness, and suddenly they become aware of a light—and it's Christ. And when they've been made aware of Him, it's one of the most remarkable moments on the planet when you see a person change from darkness to light as they respond. It is the work of the Spirit.

Greg: Right. The rest of that verse you just cited, Chuck, says that they move from darkness to light and from the power of Satan to God [Acts 26:18]. I think that people need to understand that when you engage in evangelism, you are doing something that Satan hates because you're invading his territory. The Bible says that people who are not believers are taken captive by Satan to do his will [2 Timothy 2:26]. They're blinded by the god of this world. And sometimes, maybe, we forget that there's a really huge, spiritual dynamic, like Chuck was saying, when we are all as individuals seeking to share the gospel. That's why, when you are at an event where the gospel's being proclaimed and the invitation is extended, or you yourself are extending it, you should really be praying for [those who will hear].

Dave: Yeah, that's amazing.

Chuck: Do you, at that moment . . . do you, at that moment, begin to pray in the Spirit as you're watching the Lord work? Is that what you go through, Greg? Having given the invitation, do you stand there and turn over in your mind . . . ? Let the folks know what [you're thinking] at that moment.

Greg: Well, when I give that invitation, I just feel completely dependent upon God. I feel extremely weak. People have asked me, "What is it like to stand in front of all those people? Is it exciting; is it like a real ego trip?" My response is, "It's the very opposite." Because I recognize when I stand up there, I am standing there as God's representative. I don't want to mess this up. I want to make sure what I am saying is accurate, and most importantly, biblical. And when that invitation is given, I feel so weak and so dependent upon God for the results. I just remember the verse that says, "as many as were ordained unto eternal life believed" [Acts 13:48]. In other words, now it's the work of God; it's not the work of human manipulation or cleverness. In fact, we don't even want to go there. We want to let God bring it about, so I'm really praying at that point.

Chuck: And you know what? You have to know when to be quiet. The Lord's at work, and sometimes our words invade His best message as He's communicating it to those who are struggling.

Dave: Do you think that's also the case in one-on-one, personal events?

Chuck: Oh, I absolutely do. I was going to say that a moment ago. We're talking about a crusade here, but far more often evangelism is happening in a neighborhood over coffee, at a table at a dinner between a couple of people, or when two couples have sat down together and the subject turns to Christ. Very same thing. You sense a great moment to open the subject. And just like Greg described it, you want to be so careful not to blow it or to say something that will cause another rabbit trail to occur. Because then the lost person happily goes down that other trail.

Dave: You know, there's the hook.

Chuck: Absolutely. There's no conviction there. You know that's his territory. He's comfortable there. So, you're moving him into an uncomfortable arena graciously.

Greg: It's true. Chuck, I don't know about you — being a preacher and then just sharing your faith as a Christian — but for me it's harder to do it one-on-one than it is when there's an audience listening to me. When I'm preaching it's a monologue. But when I'm sharing one-on-one, it's a dialogue. And you know the Master Communicator, Jesus Himself, modeled this so beautifully for us in John 4 with the woman at the well. Jesus asked her questions to arouse her curiosity. He listened, and He responded. It wasn't a sermon, per se, but a conversation, with give and take. He engaged her. And I think in our one-on-one sharing, we don't want to barrage people. We don't want to raise our voice and begin wagging our finger at them. It [should be] a gentle dialogue, where you're building a bridge, not burning one.

Chuck: Exactly. So true.

Dave: And let me bounce off of what we spoke about just a moment ago about maybe waiting, pausing in the conversation. When we're sharing Christ one-on-one with a person who doesn't know the Lord, what part does listening play in that dialogue?

Chuck: Oh, a big . . . a big part. Greg mentioned the Lord working with the woman at the well in John 4. Jesus also spoke to a lawyer in the middle of the street who engaged Him in a question. He answered him with a story. He was great about doing that. I think the good thing about listening is you hear what they're *not* saying—if you're really in tune. By that I don't mean you read into it something that isn't there. You really are hearing the cry of the heart.

Dave: But sometimes we get into the debate mode.

Chuck: Oh, I know.

Dave: We're two points ahead to the point that we want to make, instead of listening to what their heart is really saying.

Chuck: Yeah, I've said for years that I've never heard a testimony where this guy says, "You know, I got in an argument, and as a result of getting whipped down, I came to Christ." Nobody, nobody who is humiliated, embarrassed, put on the spot, or preached at gets excited about Christ . . . just as Greg was describing. You don't go there. You quietly and graciously, in a very winsome manner, do your best to enter their world in an authentic way so that they know, "He's really listening . . . he really cares." I have a good friend who had a rote approach to making Christ known. [One day] he was with a rather deep-thinking type of individual, and that individual realized he was talking to a guy who was just, you know, dealing with "case number five" today or "number six." And so my friend went on and on, and when he got through, the guy said to him, "Hey, why don't you just turn the record off for a minute. Let me say what I really want to ask, and then you can go back to what [you're saying]." That way of sharing is lethal in a relationship where you want to make Christ known. And Jesus never did that. His approach was always marked by variation, by creativity, by using events that were going on around them, or by the needs of a person's heart. Of course, He knew all about the heart.

Greg: Yeah. That's exactly right. He never dealt with any two people in exactly the same way. And I mentioned earlier, [look at] John 3 and 4. It's a classic example. In John 3, [Jesus speaks with] a religious man who was searching. And in John 4, [He talks to] an immoral woman who was trying to get Him off on rabbit trails about the right place to worship. He kept reeling her back in to what is essential. It's interesting how He dealt with each one, because here's the problem: you can win the argument and lose the soul. The goal here is not to win the debate; it's to win the person. And I think what Chuck is saying is so important—listening is key. Augustine once said, "Preach the gospel, and when necessary, use words." And everyone's favorite subject is themselves. So if you ask someone, "tell me about yourself," and then actually listen and pay attention, you'll hear where they're coming from. Then you can respond appropriately. It can make all the difference in the world.

Chuck: It's so true. They expect us to come on strong, and when we don't, they're disarmed. Especially when they find out that we're preachers.

Greg: Oh, yeah.

Chuck: You know it's tough when you are in ministry, and a person says, "What do you do for a living?" As soon as you say, "Well, actually I'm a minister of the gospel." Whooo! You can't imagine—his whole facial expression changes. Whereas, if you could just say, "You know, I'm a counselor," "I write books," or something like that, just to get around the subject so they won't think you're about to land on them—you're halfway there. Because they do expect the whole attack mode. And it's wonderful to surprise 'em with another plan.

Dave: Maybe we should back up half a step and talk about one of the biggest problems in personal evangelism—most believers just don't. I mean, we've got the greatest news of all. When it comes to passion, you know men; they're particularly passionate about sports teams. You know, we're "rah, rah, rah" about the Dodgers or the Dallas Cowboys or whomever it is. Or we're passionate about our favorite TV show, and we have water-cooler conversations the next day after one of the big shows. But we don't often bring up the most important thing in our lives. Why do you think that is?

Chuck: I'm going to wait for the expert on this one, and then I'll respond. What do you think, Greg?

Greg: Well, maybe it's because we're not as passionate about it as we ought to be. I'm not saying that everyone who doesn't share their faith doesn't have a passion, but I'm saying a lot of people don't have passion for the right things—for what really matters in life. There's one thing that Christians and non-Christians have in common. They're both uptight about evangelism. Nonbelievers are relatively uptight about having the gospel shared with them, and believers are often uptight about sharing it. I've heard, and I'm sure you've heard as well, Chuck, that ninety-five percent of all believers have never led another person to Christ. Now, it is the work of the Holy Spirit to bring about conversion. We all understand that. At the same time, I think a lot of times we've never "thrown the net," if you will, because we're afraid of failure. But perhaps one of the reasons we haven't thrown it is that we're afraid of success. We wouldn't know what to do. But I would encourage people that God can use every Christian to share the gospel with great effect. And I'll even add that I believe God can use every Christian to bring other people into the kingdom. And we need to be open to that.

Chuck: My answer would include that most folks have never thought through an approach ahead of time. So they aren't prepared to share Christ. And as a result, their fear is intensified. My counsel to all of our listeners today is to spend some time with a sheet of paper and a pen, and write out several approaches that would work. I mean, put yourself in the shoes of a lost person and think, *What's your world like?* and go there. Start there. Start where people are. Take them to an island across that bridge they've never taken before, but do it in a way that makes them want to travel with you. If you take that approach, most people — unless you're just really the kind of person who embarrasses people or comes on too strong — most folks will travel with you. Most folks do want to talk.

Most people do want to listen to someone who's interesting. And I would say another reason that we're hesitant to do this is that maybe we tried it a time or two and it wasn't successful. Then we tell ourselves, *Well, I'm not Greg Laurie, you know, I don't have the gift, and so that's not really my role.* But we're all to be engaged in the work of making Christ known. So, I think people ought to stop thinking about whether they're evangelists or not. You've got to realize *I know where there's good food. And I know that person I'm talking to hasn't ever tasted this kind of food. I'd like to serve him some in a way that would be attractive and appealing.* I can't imagine many people — there will be some — but not many people will say, "No, thanks. I'm just gonna live on scraps. I'm doing fine." Most folks are desperately lonely, tragically struggling with shame, guilt, heartbreak, failure, or a broken home. Or not rearing their children like they know they should, or a thousand other possibilities. Just start there; start there. Share the cracks in your own life or a struggle you're going through. People will identify with that.

Greg: One point you made, Chuck, is so powerful. You said, "Put yourself in their shoes." And that is key. Try to do that, and try to speak in English — when I say that, I mean, don't speak in "Christianese." Many times we lapse into this vocabulary that we believers understand, and we don't speak in a way that is understandable. I think that's where the personal testimony can come in. It's a great bridge builder because you don't just say, "You know the Bible says. . . ?" There's a place for that, of course. But to start with, "Let me tell you my own story of what happened to me. And let me tell you the way I used to think. This is the way I used to look at all of these things, and here's something else to consider." You know something about the person that you're about to speak to that they may not even fully know about themselves. And it's true of every person. I don't care how wealthy they are or how good-looking they are; everyone is empty inside. The Bible says that God has created this world. . . . this creation was made subject to emptiness. There's a void. There's a hole in our hearts. I know we've said it a million times, but it's true. Number two. Everyone has guilt. No matter what they try to do to get rid of it or [when they] pretend it's not there, they know it is. And another thing, everyone is afraid to die. Even though a person may seem very smug and very sure of himself, barraging me with questions, I'm reminded of the statement of C. S. Lewis when he said, "Even atheists have moments of doubt." Maybe after your conversation is over, though they may blow you out of the water, when they lay their head on the pillow at night, they'll think about that conversation. Important seeds were sown.

Dave: That's a good point. Give us just a little glimpse into the unbeliever's mind-set. I know you spend a lot of time thinking about that because you're speaking to a good many of those people in the stands at these Harvest crusades. And for believers like us who've been walking with the Lord for many years, we've got this little bubble that we live in where we've lost all relation to their perspective. Your question reminds me of a statement a good friend of mine used to make. We have known each other for years. He said, "I ask the Lord often to help me never forget what it was like outside of Christ." Now, I think that's one of the great statements you can follow up on, Greg. What is it like to be outside of Christ?

Greg: Well, Chuck, I wasn't raised in the church. My mom was married and divorced seven times. She was a full-blown alcoholic. And so I had a really weird upbringing. By the time I was seventeen, I kind of felt as though I were seventy. I felt like I'd lived so much life and I'd seen so many horrible, dark things, that even before I was a Christian, I knew the answer was not in this world. I knew it wasn't through alcohol, because I'd watched what that had done for my mom. But then, ironically, when I got into high school, I was into the party scene and drinking. I took drugs for a couple of years. They told me, "Oh hey, drugs will make you more aware." And there was some truth to that, because I became more aware of how miserable and empty I was. So for me, in becoming a Christian, much of it was a process of elimination. I knew [the answer] wasn't in alcohol. I knew it wasn't in drugs. I knew it wasn't in affluence because throughout her marriages, my mom had been married to some well-off men. I saw that lifestyle apart from anything else, and I realized that it too was empty. So when I first heard the gospel, I thought, *Is it possible this could be the truth?* There was a part of me, despite my strange upbringing, that always longed for a story with a happy ending. I loved to lose myself in movies that ended with a silver lining. And I always had this optimism in me that maybe one day life would get better. And when I heard the gospel, the cynicism kicked in immediately. *There's no way these Christians could be right. There's no way the Bible is the book we should be looking to, and Jesus Christ?* But yet at the same time, I always believed in Jesus, and I'd seen all of His movies on television. Quite frankly, that was the extent of my knowledge. But then I tried on a new thought: *What if they're right?*

Chuck: Who was the first person who, in some kind of deliberate and intelligent manner, told you the story of the good news? Who was the first one? Do you remember?

Greg: There were little bits of it in my childhood because my aunt and my uncle were Christians. In fact my uncle had a ministry in Los Angeles, the Fred Jordan Mission. That was my uncle, Fred Jordan, and Aunt Willie. And so I heard it a little bit from them. Of course I saw Billy Graham on television, and I heard a little bit there. And even in a little camp I went to when I was a kid—I heard it there—but it never resonated until I started running into friends of mine at high school whose lives had changed dramatically. And it's funny; no one invited me to a Christian meeting. I just stumbled upon one. I sort of eavesdropped on the gospel—there was a youth pastor there from Calvary Chapel. His name was Lonnie, and he shared the gospel message. For the first time, it came into focus. I got it, but I thought, *There's no way I can do it.* But by God's grace, I went forward that day, at the age of seventeen, and gave my life to the Lord.

Chuck: Was it too simple? Did it sound too easy? What was the reason that caused you to say, *Well, I hear what Lonnie's saying, but that's not my story, or that's not gonna really reach me where I am.* Did you think that?

Greg: I thought to myself, *This sounds good. I personally know a number of the people here. I used to party with some of them, and I know they're not the same people they were.* I saw the change that Christ brought into their lives, and I thought, *It's too good to be true. There's . . . there's no way. But yet . . .* I hung my head down, and I thought, *There's no way I could do it.* And this guy gave an invitation on my high school campus inviting the kids to come forward like it was a Billy Graham crusade. I thought to myself, *This is high school at lunchtime. Are you crazy? It's like social suicide to walk forward and become a Christian. But. . . .*

Chuck: Did any other kids walk forward?

Greg: Yes, yes, they really did.

Chuck: Now that had to leave an impact.

Greg: Yeah. I think as I recall, I was one of the last ones to do it. I couldn't even believe I was doing it, and when I was even praying the prayer, I was thinking to myself, *This isn't going to work for me.*

Chuck: Now, I've got to interrupt here and get a little theology in this story. This is where the Spirit of God is at work in a seventeen-year-old heart who has no background, no knowledge, and couldn't quote a verse if his life depended on it. You had no understanding of what was going to happen beyond the cross. But the Spirit of God, isn't [He] great! He does this magnetic work in a life that attracts the iron, you know, to the magnet of His pull, and you found yourself getting up out of that seat or from sitting on the ground, or wherever you were, and walking up to some guy you didn't even know.

Greg: That's right.

Chuck: Isn't that amazing? You were a seventeen-year-old with all the peer pressure, and you heard something that was so attractive — back to that magnet concept — you were drawn to do that.

Greg: Yes.

Chuck: I just think that's magnificent.

Greg: That's right.

Chuck: I'll never get over the thrill of the work of the Holy Spirit using words that explode in the mind to convince this lost person of Christ. I just think it's magnificent.

Greg: You know, Chuck, I think that you've hit on a real key: words. The Bible says it's through the foolishness *of preaching* that people believe, or more literally, *the preached thing.* You know, there's a place for Christian music. There's a place for Christian drama. There's a place for Christian movies. But people need to understand that the primary way that God brings people to Himself is through the message being communicated verbally. It may be on a radio program, like when Chuck speaks. It may be from a pulpit; it may be from a one-on-one conversation, but it is primarily through *verbal communication.* Why God has chosen this method, I don't know. But that's what He has chosen, and I'm amazed by it as well. When you are on the other side, and you share a message, sometimes you hear this story: "I was sitting in my car; I was suicidal; I heard you on the radio; and I made a commitment to Christ." [We hear] these incredible stories, and we know that God's Word doesn't return void.

Dave: That's true. You know, we're about out of time for today, which is really unfortunate, but the good news is we'll come back next time. And just to tease our audience a little bit, Chuck, next time I'm going to ask you about your personal testimony. We heard a little bit of Greg's today. Next time I want to really center in on some practical tools we can give our listeners for sharing their faith effectively and getting beyond their comfort zones—giving them a chart, a map to follow, so they don't feel like they're out in the wilderness, ready to fall flat on their faces. We'll look forward to that next time.

❧

Day Two

Dave: Well, we're glad you're with us for this special edition of the broadcast. It's a special treat because we have Pastor Greg Laurie from Harvest Christian Fellowship in Riverside, California, and Pastor Chuck Swindoll from Stonebriar Community Church in Frisco, Texas. We've got the speaker of *A New Beginning*; we've got the speaker of *Insight for Living*, and today . . .

Chuck: And we've got the announcer for both programs.

Dave: Both programs, that's me.

Greg: You bridge that gap; that's it. This is Dave Spiker sitting right here.

Chuck: That's right. You never introduce yourself, Dave.

Dave: I never do. I'm that faceless entity on both programs.

Chuck: But they know your voice.

Greg: They do. In fact, he uses this voice everywhere. We're in the restaurant earlier and, "Yes, I would like an iced tea" (*imitating Dave's voice*). I said, "Dave, don't you have just like a regular voice for when you're out and about?" He always sounds so good.

Chuck: I know.

Dave: A pastor friend of mine and I attend a Bible study on Wednesday mornings. [One day] he was talking to a friend of his, and he was going to try to get a little mileage out of the fact that he knew a radio announcer. He said, "Do you ever listen to the intros of those Christian radio broadcasts? You know, do you ever recognize the announcer on there?" He said, "Oh, they all sound the same." Then my friend said, "Well, what programs do you listen to?" "I listen to Greg Laurie and Chuck Swindoll." Of course they all sound the same!

Chuck: No kidding!

Dave: Well, when we left off last time, we'd just heard Pastor Greg's testimony of how he came to Christ on the campus of . . . that was Newport Harbor High School?

Greg: Exactly right.

Dave: In Southern California.

Chuck: Isn't that amazing, by the way? If you heard our program yesterday, you heard Greg talk about a man who was free to come and share the gospel [at his high school]. Hey, times have changed, haven't they? And he was able to even give an invitation! I was sitting there thinking, *Oh, man, try to get away with that today.*

Greg: Yeah, that's true.

Chuck: It's wonderful that you were there at that time. That's great.

Dave: Well, let me throw that same question to you, Chuck Swindoll. Tell us how you came to know Jesus Christ personally.

Chuck: Well, unlike Greg, I was reared by God-fearing parents. I was not sure of my dad's salvation until much later in his life, but my mother truly loved Christ, and I heard the name of Jesus spoken in our home from the crib as I was growing up. And so I was fortunate enough to have the benefit of being in churches where the Bible was taught and where the truth was declared. However, we know that salvation doesn't come by osmosis. You can be around it, but it doesn't make you different. I often use this illustration: you can be in a garage for three days, but it doesn't turn you into a car. You can be around people who love Christ and know Him . . . but the good news is, in this case, that there was an authenticity in my folks' lives. There was a love for our family and for the things of God. And so very early on, I guess [when I was] around five or six, I gave my heart to Christ.

Dave: Really, that early?

Chuck: Really, early on. And I really knew what I was doing. However, when you're that young, there are many things related to [salvation] that you don't know, you don't think about. The surrendering of one's will is not something that's important to you when you're five. You're just believing in Jesus so you'll go to heaven and you won't go to hell.

Dave: There was that time of rebellion when you were six.

Chuck: Actually, it came before then.

Greg: Five-and-a-half!

Chuck: Yeah, right. No, when I really got serious about spiritual things I was a teenager. I remember thinking: *This is not something I can just keep acting out. This is something that needs to make a difference.* And when I was in high school, I remember thinking, *I'm making a couple of turns in life that will go with me the rest of my years. I have to put Christ in the place where He belongs.* Call that whatever you like. It was in many ways the beginning of a serious walk with Christ — as serious as you can be, you know, in your late teen years. But I have my folks to thank for sharing the good news of Christ with me. And I have a brother who knew Christ before I did and a sister whom everybody knows, Luci, in the Women of Faith ministry. We were always close as we were growing up. She and I still talk about our mom and dad and the benefit that was ours. I never knew cursing; I never knew drinking; I never knew a wild life; I never knew divorce. It sounds really sheltered, but our world was still involved in people's lives, so I didn't think of it as sheltered. I think many of our listeners grew up in a home like that. Now, the great tragedy occurs when that lulls you to sleep. First of all, you think everybody was reared like that. Second, you don't really know the needs in the world. It took a stint in the Marine Corps for me to become aware of the depravity of humanity. Believe me, you get that in spades when you're in the military. I remember thinking — especially when I was getting ready to put my sea bag down on the floor of that Quonset hut in Okinawa, third Marine division — I remember thinking, *Before I even put these clothes in this little foot locker, I've got to determine, "Am I gonna walk with Christ or am I not?"* Because many a guy, before he ever unpacks his sea bag, is in the village with some gal, married or not; it doesn't make any difference to him. I remember thinking, *Man, I've got to get serious about this walk with Christ.* So I'm grateful. I saw the real world as I had never seen it before and may never see it again. And I had the privilege of leading seven or eight of those guys in our hut to Christ. Seven out of forty-eight Marines is a revival, guys! I want to tell you! I remember thinking, *Boy, you talk about guys watching your life; you're not only in their outfit; you're living alongside them. They're seeing you at your best and your worst.* I was grateful for the foundation that had been mine by God's grace. That [experience] really did spark my interest in evangelism.

Greg: Dave, let me just add one thing. Chuck is sharing his testimony; that's his story. And in the last program I shared mine. Everyone has a story, and one is not better than another. They're all real, but sometimes I think we may feel, well, *unless I have a dramatic testimony* — *unless I was a convict, I was a drug addict, I was a gang-banger, or whatever it is, then my testimony isn't valid.* [That isn't true], because every testimony can be boiled down to this: you were lost, you became found; you were going to hell, now you're going to heaven. Christ saved you. And regardless of what addiction you were facing, what lifestyle you were from, or if you were raised in a Christian home like Chuck — that's his story. We need to remember that when we share our testimonies, there will always be someone out there like us that will relate to our stories. Certain folks will listen to Chuck and say, "That's my story." Others will listen to my testimony and they'll say, "Oh, that's my story." Then others will hear something different. But every story is valid and should be utilized.

Chuck: Yeah, and that's why when we share Christ, we have to remember that every life we're talking to is a different life. You can even talk to twins, and they come from the same womb at the same time. . . .

Dave: In the same household.

Chuck: Yeah, same mom, same dad, same school, same church — and one could be way out-to-lunch and the other could be spiritually sensitive. They're joined at the hip, if you will, and yet they're very different. I love the fact that each one is a unique story. And God has a way of using those of us who have these different stories.

Dave: Well, Greg, I've heard you say that the testimony, our personal testimony, is perhaps the most important tool in our personal evangelism toolbox.

Greg: That's right.

Dave: In fact, I know that you helped the *New Beginning* listeners refine their testimonies into minute-long presentations of how they came to Christ. We called it the *One-Minute Message*.

Greg: Right.

Dave: Talk to us about what dynamic is at work when you're sharing your story. In essence, it's word-of-mouth advertising.

It's a personal endorsement. It's letting them see beyond the theology. It's letting them see how [Jesus] really did make a difference inside their hearts.

Greg: Yeah. You know, it's not the *most* important tool, but it's a very important tool, especially in beginning the dialogue. [Notice] I emphasize the word *dialogue*, not *monologue*. You're listening, and you're responding. I think that it shows the person you're speaking to that you have walked in their shoes, so to speak. You know what it's like to be on both sides of the fence, and now you're able to say, from the perspective of being a believer, "This is what's wonderful about knowing Christ." Everyone has a testimony, and sometimes we may think, *Well, I'm not a great theologian.* But what about that guy who was blind and said, "Look, once I was blind but now I see" [John 9:25]? It's not an excuse to avoid learning what the Scripture teaches. It's not an excuse to avoid "being prepared to give to every man an answer concerning the hope that lies within you" [1 Peter 3:15]. You know much more than most people out there who are not believers, and sharing your story is important. Ultimately, the goal is to build the bridge to the essential gospel message. I mean, if you stop with the testimony, you haven't brought home the bacon, so to speak. It's great; it opens the door and says, "Look here's what's happened to me and it can happen to you." And they might just say, "Well, that's nice, goodbye." No, wait, that was just the beginning, okay? This conversation can take place over a week, a month, a few months, you know, with a coworker, a neighbor, or something like that. But ultimately, you want to bring them home to the message of the gospel.

Chuck: You really haven't shared the gospel until you've given people something to believe. And that something is a Someone. It's all about Christ. I have found that one of the greatest ways of staying away from rabbit trails is to bring the conversation back to Christ. Bring it back to Jesus. We talked about Billy Graham earlier; he's a man we all admire. You do not hear Billy Graham speak without frequent references to the Word of God and to the person of Christ. That's why his ministry has been ignited over these years with such power. There is the presentation of the person of Christ, and by believing in Him, in Christ alone by faith alone, you can know eternal life. That's really the message in a nutshell. Now, those we're talking to have all of these foggy notions and caricatures and whatever in their minds, but if you bring them back to the Savior, you've begun to deliver the goods.

Dave: Okay, let's get really practical for our listeners right now. I know that there's somebody listening to us right now who is a committed Christian; he's been walking with the Lord for quite some time, but he's never shared the gospel with anybody. He's feeling really guilty about that right now. Let's help him. First of all, tell us what the gospel is. And Greg, I know you've made a point to say the gospel must include some things, but if we start adding on other things it kind of washes out the purity of that simple message. So, tell us, what is the gospel? In fact, let me suggest something. Can we try something? Can we experiment with something? Can we do a little role-playing?

Greg: Who are you going to be?

Dave: I'm the audience in this little melodrama. Share with Chuck. We'll switch roles in just a second. But, Chuck, you play the part of the unbeliever.

Chuck: I'm the lost person.

Dave: You're the lost person.

Greg: I'm in trouble already.

Dave: Greg, I'd like to hear you share with Chuck—this unrepentant sinner over here—what the gospel is. Just lead him through the essential elements of the gospel message.

Greg: Okay, let me backtrack for a moment. Then I'll come to that point. Because I just wanted to note that Paul says when we preach the gospel, we don't want to do it with the eloquence of man's words, lest the cross of Christ be made of no effect [1 Corinthians 1:17]. So, it needs to be somewhat streamlined. I once heard Billy Graham say in an interview with David Frost that he studied to be simple. It's important that we recognize that. We want to keep it to the essentials and not get off on rabbit trails. This is not about becoming a conservative, per se. This is not about becoming even a more moral person. I mean, those are all fine things, but let's not get the cart before the horse. It comes down to this, and this is probably what I would say to you, Chuck, if you are not a believer. I'd start with my testimony. I'd tell you a little bit about what happened to me. I would say something along the lines of, "I believe that there's a hole in each one of our hearts. And we try to fill this hole with a lot of things this world can offer. It might be experiences; it might be success; it might be accomplishments. But God loved you so much that 2,000 years ago, He sent His Son to this earth as a man. Jesus was born in a manger in Bethlehem. He lived a perfect life, and then He died on the cross for your sins [John 3:16]. Let me tell you why. The Bible says that every one of us has sinned [Romans 3:23], and sin is not just doing the *wrong* thing; it's not doing the *right* thing as well. It's not only breaking God's commandments; it's falling short of His standards. And you say, 'I'm a good person; I live a good life.' But the problem is that none of us are good enough. Jesus said, 'Be perfect as My Father in heaven is perfect' [Matthew 5:48]. And I'm not perfect; nor are you. But God loved us so much, He put His judgment that should have come upon you and upon me, upon His Son who died in our place and shed His blood for us. It wasn't nails that held Jesus to that cross that day; it was love for you. Because He loved you so much, He died in your place. If you will turn from your sin and put your faith in Jesus, He'll fill the hole in your heart. You'll go to heaven when you die; He will take away your guilt; and He'll give you purpose and meaning in your life."

Chuck: Well, Greg, you're acting like I'm a guy that's been out killing people, but I . . . I pay my taxes, and I'm . . . I'm good to my wife. I have four kids, and they know I love them. I mean, I could tell you about a sinner who's living next door to me. Man, you ought to see the way he lives. I mean compared to him, Greg, I don't think I'm in that category you just described. I don't think I'm there.

Greg: You are a nice guy, Chuck. I like you. But it's not about just being good, you see, because we all have broken God's commandments. The Bible says, "For all have sinned and fall short of the glory of God" [Romans 3:23]. And the Bible also says this, "To him that knows to do good and does not do it, it is sin" [James 4:17]. So we all have broken God's commandments and fallen short of His standards. And one sin is enough to keep you out of heaven. You see, the Bible says that if we offend one point of the law, we're guilty of all of it [James 2:10]. Let me ask you a question. Have you ever told a lie in your entire life?

Chuck: Yeah, I have. I've . . . I've lied before.

Greg: Okay. Have you ever taken the Lord's name in vain?

Chuck: Yes, I have. I've done that.

Greg: Okay, you've already broken two of the commandments. I could keep going down the list. And one of those is enough to keep you out of heaven. Listen, if all good people could get to heaven, why would God have poured His wrath out upon His Son—why would He have had to die in our place? Don't you think that if there was another way that this could be accomplished, God would not have taken such drastic measures? You can tell the depth of a well by how much rope has to be lowered. Look at how much rope God lowered, so to speak. Look at the sacrifice He made so you could come into a relationship with Him.

Chuck: Yeah, but what about the person that's never heard? I mean, I've been to Africa, and I saw a lot of folks there who have never once heard anything like this. Are you telling me that God, a God of love, will send those people to hell? Because, I mean, they've never heard about Jesus. Are you over there telling them about Him?

Greg: Well, I actually have been to Africa, and I have preached there, and I know that Chuck Swindoll's radio program is heard over there so maybe that will help to reach some of them . . . That's another subject; I don't think *A New Beginning* has . . .

Chuck: You know what's great? That is a really bad answer.

Greg: That's not my answer; I'm just pandering to you right now because I'm intimidated, and then you ask me these questions!

Chuck: I'm trying to make life a little harder for you, because you've got a perfect story over there — I have to mess it up!

Greg: No, it's good. And those are . . .

Dave: You wait, the tables will be turned in just a minute.

Chuck: I know, I know. That's what I'm afraid of, so I'm gonna be a little nicer here. But actually, Greg, I like you. You're a good guy.

Greg: But the question is one that's often asked, and my response is that the Bible tells us that God has revealed Himself through nature [Romans 1:20]. He's revealed Himself through the human conscience. Deep down inside, we know what is right and wrong. Listen, nobody wants a person to be saved and forgiven of their sin and go to heaven more than God Himself. Here's what it comes down to. Chuck, you have heard the gospel; you do know what it says; you do know what you need to do about Jesus Christ. Instead of worrying so much about people who *haven't* heard it, you need to be thinking about yourself, because you *have* heard it, and you'll be held accountable for what you have heard.

Chuck: Well, let me ask you then. Because I have heard and you've spelled it out very clearly, what exactly do I have to do? I mean, when I go to bed tonight, do I pray or . . . or do I tell my wife that we ought to be more religious and start going to church? What should I do? How do I come into this new relationship you're talking about?

Greg: Well, the Bible says, "If you will confess your sin, He is faithful and just to forgive your sin and cleanse you from all unrighteousness" [1 John 1:9]. Let me break that down for you. The word *confess* means "to agree with." It means that you have to agree with God. You need to see yourself the way God sees you—as someone who has fallen short of His standards, someone whom He loves and wants to forgive. So, you have to say first of all, "I'm a sinner, and I admit it." Then you need to be willing to turn from that sin. The Bible says to repent and be converted. The word *repent* means "to change your direction." It's a change of mind, and it's a change of direction. The Bible says, "God has commanded people everywhere to repent" [Mark 1:15]. You need to be willing to turn from your sin. This is really important. You have to put your faith in Jesus Christ and Jesus Christ alone to save you. Then you need to ask Him into your life, and you do that through prayer. It's as simple as saying, "Lord, I know I've sinned, and I want You to come into my life." I'll just sort of digress for a moment and explain what I often do here. If I'm actually at the point where Chuck just asked me that question, what I would try to do if you really asked me that, is try to pull in the net. You want to at least make an attempt to say, "Could I pray with you right now. Would you give me the privilege of leading you in a prayer?" And if they're uncomfortable with that, and sometimes people are, I'll just say, "Look, then just say to God, 'I'm sorry for my sin. I turn from it now. I put my faith in Jesus Christ. Lord, make Yourself real to me.'" And I'm confident that God is going to reveal Himself and transform a person that really is coming to Him, because He has said, "You will seek Me and find Me" [Jeremiah 29:13]. But I would actually try to do it on the spot if I could.

Chuck: Yeah, that's very good.

Dave: That's good stuff. Well, Chuck, I don't want to be completely redundant and go through the whole melodrama again, but let me ask you, from a theologian's perspective, what parts of the gospel need to be there for the gospel to be the gospel?

Chuck: Well, 1 Corinthians 15 spells it out in simple and succinct terms—"Christ died for our sins, according to the Scriptures, and He was buried." Paul mentions this as proof of Jesus's death. After dying for our sins, He was buried. Then the Scripture states, "and He rose again from the dead and was seen by . . . " [1 Corinthians 15:4–8] and it describes a number of times He was seen. Paul mentions *that* as proof of His resurrection. Believing the good news concerning Christ is believing that His death provided the complete and sufficient payment for my sins. I don't have to add anything to it. I don't have to bring good works, I don't have to promise to go to church for a year, I don't have to promise to give up my sins, and I don't have to promise to clean up my act. All of those things will occur with the passing of time. To believe in Jesus—He died for me paying the complete price for my sin, and He was raised from the dead, miraculously and bodily *for me*, personally. By believing in Him, I have entrusted my life to Him, and He has in turn given me eternal life. There's a great word for this; you mentioned theology, and I love this term. It's called *justification*. It doesn't mean "just as if I'd never sinned." I hear that sometimes, and I cringe a little. It's deeper than that because we have sinned. It's not "just as if I hadn't." The problem is, I have sinned, big time. And so, justification is the sovereign act of God whereby He declares righteous the believing sinner.

Dave: Not just guiltless, but *righteous*.

Chuck: Right, right. He *declares* righteous the believing sinner while we are still in a sinning state. Isn't that a great thought!

Greg: That is.

Chuck: He declares us to be righteous. He doesn't make us righteous. That's a process of growing. That's *sanctification*. But at that moment, because we have believed, He declares us righteous in His eyes—as righteous as His Son, while we are still in a sinning state. Isn't that magnificent?

Dave: It's worth that twenty-five-cent theological word.

Chuck: It's worth a seminary education to learn that, I'll tell you. And it puts skin on what Greg explains so clearly. It's not just works you need to work on. People are under this delusion that says, *If I could just be good enough, or if I could just give up enough of this, or if I could just get rid of . . .* It's none of that. You can't do enough of anything. Christ did it all. And as a result of trusting Him who took my place—I should have been the one nailed to a cross, the way I've lived my life—but because He was nailed there for me, I can be justified, declared righteous by God's grace. You see, it's the grace message. And Greg is such a great messenger of it, I hesitate to mention the obvious. But the good news is that Christ has done all of this for people who don't deserve it, who can never earn it, who will never be able to repay. He comes to us. We don't come to Him. He seeks us out long before we seek Him. He brings to our side somebody who knows the truth. He gets to us, to our attention, by this radio program or that television program. Or by that verse of Scripture that somehow I come across and read, or I hear it, and I say, "Thank You, Christ, for coming into my life." That's grace. That's grace.

Dave: Greg, we want to follow up on what we mentioned earlier—that the gospel must include some things, and that there are other things that some people try to add on to the gospel that dilute the message. What should we make sure we stay away from?

Greg: Well, I think that the idea is just simply keeping to the main thing. The main thing is to keep the main thing the main thing. Chuck has identified what that main thing is; it's the death of Jesus Christ. It's His resurrection from the dead; it's the lost person putting his or her faith in Him alone for salvation. *Gospel* comes from a phrase that means "good news." But we do have to tell people they're sinners. The one thing that concerns me today is that I hear people preaching the so-called gospel, and it goes something along the lines of this: "Listen, all you have to do is just ask Jesus in and pray this little prayer, and you're forgiven, and off you go." The problem I have with that is I don't think people understand that they are putting their faith in Christ and committing to follow Him from that point on. It's almost as though He's a nice additive to one's life. He will give you a little more spring in your step, make your teeth a little whiter, and maybe you'll be a little more successful. I think we need to proclaim the *exclusivity* of Jesus Christ—we live in a day where even Christians don't fully understand that Jesus really is the *only* way to the Father. I've even heard some well-meaning but obviously misled believers say something along the lines of, "Well, Jesus Christ is the answer for me. Now somebody else may have his own path or his own beliefs, and God will give him eternal life as well. We're all on the same road." No, we aren't. We have to understand that Christ and Christ alone saves us. And when I proclaim it, I leave out things that are peripheral. Because the problem is, sometimes people know Christians more for what we're against than what we're for. So when I'm giving an evangelistic message, I'm not going to hammer on the evils of abortion, on a person who's living in adultery, or on a homosexual lifestyle. I mean, I may address it to some degree, but I'm not going to make that my main point. Because, see, here's my goal: I want to reach the person who is trapped in a homosexual lifestyle or the young girl who's thinking of getting an abortion. Or if she's had one, I want to let her know that there's forgiveness from God if she'll bring that sin to Jesus. I want to reach the person in the state that they're in and not drive them away because they've been hammered on so much that they haven't seen [Jesus's] compassion. I mean, look at the woman at the well. She was an adulteress, and our Lord acknowledged that as she played a little verbal game with Him. But she could see the love that He had for her. He even conversed with her in her language. You know, Jews didn't speak with Samaritans, as she so properly pointed out. She was alienated from other folks in that city because of the life she had lived, drawing water in the middle of the afternoon instead of early in the day as the others would. Jesus reached out to her. I think that we want to reach the person and bring him or her to Christ first, and then the changes will come, as Chuck has said. And that's what I mean about leaving certain things out. Let's not get the cart before the horse. Let's give them the main message of who Jesus is, what He has said, and how they can come into a relationship with Him. The Bible says that it is the goodness of God that brings us to repentance [Romans 2:4].

Chuck: When he tells his story or describes it that way, it reminds me of a time in my own ministry when I realized that it was time for me to preach a message about the gospel. I said to Cynthia one afternoon, "You know what I'm going to do? I'm going to bring two messages sort of back to back. One is 'How Does a Person Become Born Again?'" I remember giving the simplest kind of message, a "Theology 101." I mean, you learn to do this when you're in your first year of seminary. I remember breaking it down, not using any two-bit words, not in any way trying to impress. I spoke to our congregation about why and how a person becomes a Christian. How do you get across that bridge from lostness to being saved—from the darkness to light? After that, I delivered a message called "Now That You've Been Born Again, What Is Involved in Growing?" Those two messages kind of went back-to-back, and to my surprise there was an enormous interest in both. And I want to say to all of those who are listening who happen to be fellow preachers, it might have been a long time since you delivered a couple of messages like these. I urge you to do that. It will make a difference in your congregation, I can assure you.

Dave: Well, before our time runs completely out, I do want to touch on the topic of that second message you just mentioned. We've talked a lot today about the essence of the gospel. There was a great dialogue between you. But we absolutely must talk about how we follow up when we present it. When we present the gospel, and they say, "Yes, I want to pray to accept Christ," we don't just say, "Great, have a nice day. Be warm and filled," and go on our way. What do we do?

Chuck: I think one of the first things we must do is assure them that they are indeed in the family of God. The enemy goes to work right away with a brand-new believer. He tries to convince that person once they've left you, and they're alone, or they're with their friends, "You know what, that's a bunch of religious hogwash. That didn't make any difference in you . . . you're gonna go back with the gang and whatever." No, they need reassurance. So, I try before I even leave their presence to say, "Let us pause right here. Now that you've made [this decision], let me assure you of something." And I'll show them from the Scriptures that God has given them eternal life: "He who has the Son has the life; he who doesn't have the Son does not have the life" [John 3:36]. You have the life because you have the Son. Jesus said, "I am the way, the truth, and the life; no one comes to the Father, but through Me" [John 14:6]. You have come to God through Christ. You are in the family. I want to drive that home. The second thing I want to do is to help them know what to do with their sin. Because they will be shocked when day after tomorrow, if not tomorrow, they fall back into old habits.

Dave: They may be thinking what Greg thought when he first accepted Christ, *I guess it doesn't work for me.*

Chuck: Exactly. That's the first thing you think, and that's the enemy at work. You know what? It really was, *You weren't sincere enough,* or *you didn't give up enough.* Or *this guy talking to you, you ought to know the way . . . the real truth.* And they'll go on and on. So you need to understand, once you know that you're in the family, that you will still have times when you fall. There will still be moments where you think wrong thoughts, you say wrong words, and you do wrong things. Listen to [I John 1:9]. I call it the Christian's bar of soap. It's the whole idea of coming to Christ, and agreeing with Him: "If we confess our sins, [God] is faithful and righteous to forgive us our sins" — those are the things we named — "and to cleanse us from all unrighteousness" — those are the things we don't name. Those are the things we don't know about. We call them "sins of commission" and "sins of omission." He'll cover both. You come to Him, and you tell

Him. Third, tell Him that this was wrong; agree with Him, and say, "Thank You for forgiving me. Help me as I begin to live this life to learn how to live it in Your strength and power." Next, they need to learn about the source of power. That's the work of the Holy Spirit. That will take a little while for them to grasp. But they need to know they're not walking in their own strength, and they now have a new power, now that they're in the family of God. They have a new name, and the name is *Jesus*—Christ is at work in me. They need to know about the fruit of the Spirit and how the Lord wants to control their lives, which is called His *filling*, and how He can fill them and enable them to live the life of Christ. I remember reading from one of my mentors, "The life that Christ lived qualified Him for the death that He died. And the death that Christ died qualifies *us* for the life that He lived." So this empowered life, made possible by the Holy Spirit, is something that's new to them. They need to understand; it's theirs to claim.

Dave: Pastor Greg, what about following up. Let's say a coworker has just accepted Christ on the lunch hour. What do we tell him or her about things like reading the Bible, prayer, attending a church, fellowship, and things like that? What words do we need to share with him or her in that respect?

Greg: Well, I think we need to engage in a little bit of show and tell. By that, I mean we need to tell them what to do. Obviously, every new believer needs to begin to read the Bible. I often encourage new believers to read the Gospel of John. That's a good place to start. And then he should work his way right through the New Testament and on through the Bible. That is essential. And then, of course, praying—learning to converse with God, to commune with God, to communicate with God, to listen to God—and then being involved in a church. This comes to the part about *showing*. You need to model it for them, and more to the point, you need to help them. When people are new in their faith, they're introduced to this new world that's exciting. Like Chuck was saying, the enemy is there, attacking in full force, not unlike he did in the Garden of Eden. Satan challenged God's Word, *Did God really say what you thought He said?* In the same way, he comes to the new believer and says, *Do you really think you are saved?* So they need reassurance; they need a friend. They need someone to take them under his or her wing and help them to see what it is to live the Christian life. And I can't encourage believers enough. Find yourself a young believer. The best way to do that is if by God's grace you can lead someone to Christ. Then do it on your own. But if you can't, go talk to your pastor and say, "Pastor, can you introduce me to a young believer in the church. I would like to help him or her."

Chuck: That's a great idea. That's a great idea.

Greg: Be an Aquila or Priscilla as they were with Apollos [Acts 18]. Take that person under your wing, and take him to church. I'm so thankful someone did this for me, going back to my own story. I'd accepted Christ; I had no idea what I had done. No one gave me a Bible to read. I didn't know I should go to church or pray or do anything. In fact that weekend I went out to take drugs because I had planned to do that on that weekend. And this is the grace of God. While I was getting ready to go, that same still, small voice I'd heard the day before simply said, "You don't need that anymore." And I realized that drugs were now a part of my past — not my present or future — and I closed that door. I came back the next Monday to school. Thank God, a guy named Mark came up to me and said, "I saw you go forward and accept Christ. I want to take you to church with me." He started helping me learn what it meant to be a Christian. It made all the difference in my life. So we need to do that for somebody else. Not only will it be a blessing for a new believer, but I think it could revive Christians as they rediscover truth they've forgotten.

Dave: That's good stuff. Well, I'm thinking that in just a minute or two we're gonna hear some Harleys rev out in the parking lot.

Chuck: Oh. Well, we're back at it. Watch out for your speed limit there, Greg, okay?

Greg: Okay, you lead Chuck. I'll follow.

Chuck: Yeah, right!

Dave: I want to thank both of you guys for riding your Harleys into the studio today and being with us on this special edition of the program. It's been an outstanding time, and I think our listeners have really been given a better glimpse of their privilege of sharing the gospel and how to go about it. It was a good dialogue.

Chuck: Thank you, Greg, for all you mean to the family, and thank you for your faithfulness over many years.

Greg: Chuck, thank you for all that you mean to me and to so many others out there. I listen to your program every day, love it, and I am privileged to sit here in this studio. Thanks for sitting here with me and having this time.

Chuck: Oh, it's been wonderful. It's been great. Can I pray?

Dave: Please.

Chuck: Thank You, Father, for a few moments to talk about things that are on Your heart. Thank You for the truth You've given us in a world that's moving rapidly in the wrong direction because it's lost its way. Help us to know how to point the way and to live the way and then to get out of the way so that Christ can make a dent and a difference in the lives of those who've never met Him. Remind us that it's never too late to start doing what is right. And we pray for those who've never trusted Christ, that they will begin today a walk that will lead them from time to eternity and from darkness to light. In the name of Jesus, amen.

Chapter 2

Gospel Basics —
"Mr. Smith, Meet Your Substitute"
by Chuck Swindoll

When Peter Marshall preached, people listened. Even if they didn't believe what he said. Even when they said they were not interested. The man refused to be ignored.

Who can fully explain it? There was something about his winsome, contagious style that made it impossible for people not to listen. Even when he became chaplain of the United States Senate and prayed more than he preached, his prayers became legendary. Ask those who were fortunate enough to have heard him. They'll tell you that everywhere Marshall preached, crowds gathered. Even if it were raining or snowing outside, the main floor and balconies would be full, packed with people, and many others who could not find a seat were willing to stand and listen as he spoke the truth of the living God.

Peter Marshall was Scottish, but his popularity went deeper than his Scottish brogue. And it certainly was more than just a charming personality or his well-timed humor that would win a hearing. The man had a way with men as well as women. He was admired by both. A man's man and yet a sensitive touch. At times one would swear he was more a poet than a preacher. He wasn't extemporaneous. To the surprise of many, Marshall *read* his sermons, considered a no-no by most professors of homiletics. But I suppose if one could read like Peter Marshall, who really cared if he broke that rule?

A contemporary of Marshall's said it best with this terse analysis:

> What Peter Marshall says, you never forget. . . . But it isn't *how* he says it, so much as it is *what* he says, you never forget. . . . He has a gift for word pictures, for little dramas and folksy incidents; he takes you out on the road to Galilee and makes you think you belong there, and he brings you back sharply to Main Street. He never preaches over your head.[1]

Perhaps that, more than any other single ingredient, was the secret of the man's success. He certainly had the ability to go much deeper, but he purposely restrained himself. He was always cognizant of his audience. Because he was from an impoverished background, he understood the common man and woman. So he spoke in plain terms, colorful to be sure, and dramatic at times; but people never had trouble connecting with what Peter Marshall was saying.

Listen to a part of one of his sermons:

> Our country is full of Joneses, and they all have problems of one kind or another. "All God's chillun' got trouble these days."
>
> The Church has always contended that God can solve these problems through the individual's personal fellowship with a living Lord.
>
> Let's put the question bluntly, as bluntly as Mr. Jones would put it.

Can you and I really have communion with Christ as we would with earthly friends?

Can we know personally the same Jesus whose words are recorded in the New Testament, Who walked the dusty trails of Galilee two thousand years ago?

I don't mean can we treasure His words or try to follow His example or imagine Him.

I mean, is He really alive? Can we actually meet Him, commune with Him, ask His help for our every-day affairs?

The Gospel writers say "yes." A host of men and women down the ages say "yes." And the church says "yes." [2]

Appropriately, he entitled that sermon "Mr. Jones, Meet the Master." I have hitched onto the man's idea by choosing a similar title for this chapter: "Mr. Smith, Meet Your Substitute." I figure that Mr. Jones has been picked on long enough. We need to give Jones a break. So, Mr. Smith, this is for you . . . as well as for your wife . . . and the Johnsons, the Franklins, the Clarks, the Parkers, or whatever your name may be. Because I'm writing to the common man or woman today who happens to find himself or herself in the same precarious predicament.

The predicament is called sin. And that's why you need a substitute.

FOUR MAJOR ISSUES

$\mathcal{L}$et's talk about that "why" issue.

The sixth book in the New Testament is the book of Romans. In the third chapter of that book (which is actually a letter originally written to some people who lived in Rome, Italy, in the first century), you may be surprised to hear that your biography is included. It doesn't actually include your name or your place of residence, but it does tell the story of your personal life. The stuff it mentions isn't very attractive, I should warn you, but it is the truth. And so, Mr. Smith, this is your life. I mentioned it earlier, but it bears repeating.

Our Condition: Totally Depraved

What then? Are we better than they? Not at all; for we have already charged that both Jews and Greeks are all under sin; as it is written,

"There is none righteous, not even one;
There is none who understands,
There is none who seeks for God;
All have turned aside, together they have
    become useless;
There is none who does good,
There is not even one.
Their throat is an open grave,
With their tongues they keep deceiving,
The poison of asps is under their lips;
Whose mouth is full of cursing and bitterness;
Their feet are swift to shed blood,
Destruction and misery are in their paths,

And the path of peace they have not known.
There is no fear of God before their eyes."

> Now we know that whatever the Law says, it speaks to those who are under the Law, so that every mouth may be closed, and all the world may become accountable to God; because by the works of the Law no flesh will be justified in His sight; for through the Law comes the knowledge of sin. . . . For all have sinned and fall short of the glory of God. (Romans 3:9–20, 23)

Honestly, now, does that sound like your life? Is that a fairly apt description of the inner you . . . down where nobody else can look? I think so. How do I know? Because it describes me, too. To borrow from my earlier comment, you and I are "blue all over." Even when we try to hide it, even when we put on our sophisticated best, it comes out when we least expect it.

Maybe you heard about the large commercial jet that was flying from Chicago to Los Angeles. About half an hour after takeoff, the passengers on board heard a voice over the loud speaker. "Good morning, ladies and gentlemen. This is a recording. You have the privilege of being on the first wholly electronically controlled jet. This plane has no pilot or copilot and no flight engineer because they are no longer needed. But do not worry, nothing can possibly go wrong, go wrong, go wrong, go wrong, go wrong, go wrong. . . ."

God's Character: Infinitely Holy

Next, my friend Smith, I should mention something that will only add insult to injury. God is righteous, perfect, and infinitely holy. That's His standard. It is sometimes called "glory" in the New Testament. We looked earlier at Romans 3:23. Let me paraphrase it:

For all have sinned [that's our condition] and fall short
of the perfection, holiness, righteousness, and glory
[that's His standard] of God.

Unlike all humanity, God operates from a different level of
expectation. His existence is in the realm of absolute perfection.
He requires the same from others. Whoever hopes to relate to Him
must be as righteous as He is righteous. How different from us!
To relate to me you don't have to be perfect. In fact, if you act like
you are, I get very uncomfortable. "Just be what you are," we say.
But God is not like that. God doesn't shrug, wink, and say, "Ah,
that's okay."

Let me put it another way. God's triangle is perfect. And in order
for us to fellowship with Him, our triangles must be congruent. The
sides and the angles must match. So must the space within. Perfection requires matching perfection.

Ah, there's the rub! We have sinned and fallen short of the
perfection of God. No one qualifies as perfect. Don't misunder-
stand; there are times that our goodness is astounding. We take
great strides; we produce great achievements. We may even surprise ourselves with periodic times of goodness, gentleness, and
compassion. But "perfect"? Never. Or "infinitely holy"? How about
"pure"? No, only God is those things. Romans 3:21 calls God's perfection, holiness, and purity "the righteousness of God [that] has
been manifested, being witnessed by the Law and the Prophets."
Compared to *that* standard, all humans come up short.

The New Living Translation puts it like this:

For the more we know God's law, the clearer it becomes
that we aren't obeying it. (Romans 3:20)

Isn't that the truth? He is perfect and spotless white. Not a taint of gray. Not a hint of blue. And along comes our blue rectangle, trying to work its way into that perfect, holy, and pure triangle. And the two just won't match! There is no way, Mr. Smith, that we can match His righteousness.

Our Need: A Substitute

Here we are, sinners by birth, sinners by nature, sinners by choice, trying to reach and attain a relationship with the holy God who made us. And we fall short. We can't make it because we're spiritually crippled. In fact, the New Testament teaches that we're "dead in trespasses and sin."

What do we need? Let me put it plain and simple, Mr. Smith; we need help outside ourselves.

We need some way to become clean within so that we can relate to a God who is perfect. Scripture says, "God is light, and in Him there is no darkness at all" (1 John 1:5). If we hope to know God, walk with God, and relate to God, we must be able to stand the scrutiny of that kind of light. But our light is out. We're all dark, and He is all light. In his immortal hymn, Charles Wesley envisioned us in a dark dungeon, chained and helpless—

> Long my imprisoned spirit lay
> Fast bound in sin and nature's night.[3]

We can't get out of the dungeon, not even if we try. Our own sin holds us in bondage. We need someone to rescue us from the hole. We need an advocate in the courtroom of justice. We need someone who will present our case. We need someone to be our substitute. So God provided the Savior.

God's Provision: A Savior

> [We] are justified freely by his grace through the
> redemption that came by Christ Jesus. God presented
> him as a sacrifice of atonement, through faith in his
> blood. He did this to demonstrate his justice, because
> in his forbearance he had left the sins committed
> beforehand unpunished—he did it to demonstrate
> his justice at the present time, so as to be just and
> the one who justifies those who have faith in Jesus.
> (Romans 3:24–26 NIV)

Isn't that great news? Mr. Smith, you have just been introduced to
your Substitute. He is Christ, the sinless and perfect Son of God. He
is the One who accomplished your rescue. It occurred on a cross. It
was effective because He was the only One who could qualify as our
substitute before God. Sin requires a penalty—death—in order
for God's righteous demands to be satisfied. The ransom must be
paid. And Christ fills that role to perfection. You and I need to
be washed. We need to be made sparkling clean. And God can't give
up on His plan, for He hates sin. Being perfect, He cannot relate to
sinful things. He couldn't even if He tried, because His nature is
repelled by sin. Sin calls for judgment. And that is why the cross
is so significant. It became the place of judgment. It was there the
price was paid in full.

In verse 24 of Romans 3, the term *justified* appears. Let's work
with that word a few moments. It does not simply mean "just as
if I'd never sinned." That doesn't go far enough! Neither does it
mean that God makes me righteous so that I never sin again.
It means "to be declared righteous." Justification is God's merciful

act whereby He declares righteous the believing sinner while he is still in a sinning state. He sees us in our need, wallowing around in the swamp of our sin. He sees us looking to Jesus Christ and trusting Him completely by faith to cleanse us from our sin. And though we come to Him with all of our needs and in all of our darkness, God says to us, "Declared righteous! Forgiven! Pardoned!" Wesley caught the significance of all this as he completed that same stanza:

> Thine eye diffused a quick'ning ray,
> I woke, the dungeon flamed with light;
> My chains fell off, my heart was free;
> I rose, went forth and followed Thee.[4]

I like the way Billy Graham imagines all this:

Picture a courtroom. God the Judge is seated in the judge's seat, robed in splendor. You are arraigned before Him. He looks at you in terms of His own righteous nature as it is expressed in the moral law. He speaks to you:

GOD: John (or) Mary, have you loved Me with all your heart?

JOHN/MARY: No, Your Honor.

GOD: Have you loved others as you have loved yourself?

JOHN/MARY: No, Your Honor.

GOD: Do you believe you are a sinner and that Jesus died for your sins?

JOHN/MARY: Yes, Your Honor.

GOD: Then your penalty has been paid by Jesus Christ on the cross and you are pardoned. . . . Because Christ is righteous, and you believe in Christ, I now declare you legally righteous.

Can you imagine what a newspaperman would do with this event?

SINNER PARDONED — GOES TO LIVE WITH JUDGE

It was a tense scene when John and Mary stood before the Judge. [He] transferred all of the guilt to Jesus Christ, who died on a cross for John and Mary.

After John and Mary were pardoned the Judge invited them to come to live with Him forever.

The reporter on such a story like that would never be able to understand the irony of such a scene, unless he had been introduced to the Judge beforehand and knew His character.

Pardon and Christ's righteousness come to us only when we totally trust ourselves to Jesus as our Lord and Savior. When we do this, God welcomes us into His intimate favor. Clothed in Christ's righteousness we can now enjoy God's fellowship.[5]

All of that is included in what it means to be justified. I come to Him in all my need. I am hopelessly lost, spiritually dead. And I present myself to Christ just as I am. I have nothing to give that would earn my way in. If I could I would, but I can't. So the only way I can present myself to Him in my lost condition is by faith. Coming in my need, expressing faith in His Son who died for me, I understand that God sees me coming by faith and admitting my sinfulness. At that epochal moment, He declares me righteous.

On occasion I think of the cross as a sponge . . . a "spiritual sponge" that has taken the sins of mankind—past, present, and future—and absorbed them all. At one awful moment, Christ bore our sins, thus satisfying the righteous demands of the Father, completely and instantaneously clearing up my debt. My sin is forgiven. My enslavement is broken. I am set free from sin's power once and for all. *Redemption*, another significant word in verse 24, also occurs. I am set at liberty so as never to come back to the slave market of sin—never again in bondage to it. And remember, the rescue occurred because of what *Christ* did—not because of what I did.

I love the way Romans 3:28 reads:

> For we maintain that a man is justified by faith apart from works of the Law.

I remember hearing a seasoned Bible teacher say, "Man is incurably addicted to doing something for his own salvation." What a waste! Scripture teaches that salvation is a by-faith, not-by-works transaction.

In Romans 4:4–5, this is made ever so clear:

> Now to the one who works, his wage is not credited as a favor, but as what is due. But to the one who does not work, but believes in Him who justifies the ungodly, his faith is credited as righteousness.

Just think of your paycheck, Mr. Smith. When your boss or someone from your boss's office brings you your paycheck, you take it. You take it, I might add, without a great deal of gratitude. You don't drop to your knees and say, "Oh, thank you—thank you so very much for this gift." You probably grab the check and don't give much thought to saying thanks. Why? Because you *earned* it. You worked *hard* for it. Now, if your boss attaches a bonus of a thousand bucks (and maybe even adds, "Though you're dropping in your efficiency, I want you to know I love you"), wouldn't that be great? That would be a miracle! There's a great difference between a wage and a gift.

God looks at us in all of our need and He sees nothing worth commending. Not only are we dropping in our spiritual efficiency, we have no light, no holiness. We're moving in the opposite direction, despising Him, living in a dungeon of sin, habitually carrying out the lifestyle of our sinful nature. Realizing our need, we accept His miraculous, eternal bonus — the gift of His Son. And in grace, our dungeon "flamed with light." You and I didn't even deserve the light, yet He gave it to us as an unmerited gift. Look again at verse 5:

> But to the one who does not work, but believes in Him who justifies the ungodly, his faith is credited as righteousness.

I love that verse! Because there's no way you and I can get any credit. We're bound in a dungeon, lost in ourselves. We don't even know where to find the light. Even when we try, we are like the line out of the country-western song; we "look for love in all the wrong places."

This reminds me of the story I read about a drunk down on all fours late one night under a streetlight. He was groping around on the ground, feeling the cement, peering intently at the little cracks. And a friend drives up and says, "Sam, what are you doing there?" Sam answers, "I lost my wallet." So the friend gets out of his car, walks over, gets down on his hands and knees with him, and they both start looking. Neither one can find it. Finally the friend says to the drunk buddy:

"Are you sure you lost the wallet here?"

"Of course not! I dropped it half a block over there."

"Then why are we looking here?"

"Because there's no *streetlight* over there."

Mr. Smith, I'm going to level with you. I know you fairly well, even though we've never met. You read these words about the *gift* of eternal life and you simply cannot fathom them, so you won't take them. I mean, you've got your pride, so you will reject them. I can even imagine your reluctance: "Too good to be true, Chuck. Sounds great. Looks good in a book. And it's definitely an intriguing idea. Who wouldn't want to tell people that? But if I get into heaven, I'll earn it on my own."

Well, let me give you just a little logic to wrestle with. If you plan to work your way in, how much work is enough work to guarantee that you have made it? And if it's something you work for, why does God say in His Book that it's for "the one who does *not* work, but believes . . ."?

Let me spell it out:

God's Character:	Infinitely Holy
Our Condition:	Totally Depraved
Our Need:	A Substitute
God's Provision:	A Savior

When God provided the Savior, He said to each one of us, "Here is my Gift to you." How often, when folks hear that, they shake their heads and mumble, "I can't believe it."

In 2 Corinthians 5:20, we find these words:

> Therefore, we are ambassadors for Christ, as though God were making an appeal through us; we beg you on behalf of Christ, be reconciled to God.

That's the message of this chapter in a nutshell. I beg you . . . be reconciled to God. Watch that barrier crumble, the one between you and God, as you step across by faith. Look at the next verse.

> He made Him who knew no sin to be sin on our behalf, so that we might become the righteousness of God in Him.

Now, let me identify the pronouns:

> He [God, the Father] made Him [God, the Son] who knew no sin to be sin on our behalf [that happened at the cross], so that we [the sinner] might become the righteousness of God in Him [Christ].

Let's boil it down:

God:	The Righteous
Christ:	The Sacrifice
We:	The Sinner
Christ:	The Life

How? The cross.

But how can the sinner in the black hole of his need ever know God in the spotless white of all His righteousness? Verse 21 tells us. By coming to know Him who knew no sin, the one who became sin on our behalf. Put your pride in your pocket, Mr. Smith. You need a substitute. You need a defense attorney . . . an eternal advocate. And in Christ—and Christ alone—you've got one.

THREE CRUCIAL QUESTIONS

Seems to me there are three crucial questions we must answer. Each has a two-word answer.

Question	Answer
1. Is there any hope for lost sinners?	Yes, Christ.
2. Isn't there any work for a seeker to do?	No, believe.
3. Is there any way for the saved to lose the gift?	No, never!

Now let me spell that out.

First question: Is there any hope for lost sinners? Yes, Christ. Not Christ and the church. Not Christ and good works. Not Christ and sincerity. Not Christ and giving up your sins. Not Christ and trying really hard. Not Christ and baptism, Christ and christening, Christ and morality, or Christ and a good family. No! Christ (period). Otherwise, it's works. He died for our sins and was placed in the grave as proof of His death. He rose from the dead bodily, miraculously, in proof of His life beyond. If you believe that He died and rose for you, you have eternal life. It's a gift.

Second question: Isn't there any work for a seeker to do? Don't I have to add to it? Answer: No (period). Believe!

One of my favorite illustrations of the importance of believing and not working is to consider a nice meal you and I enjoy together. You invite me over. I come to your home. We have planned this for quite some time, and you've worked hard in the kitchen. You have prepared my favorite meal. You are thrilled because you have a great recipe. And I'm happy because it's going to be a delightful evening with you. I knock on your front door. I'm starved. We sit down together at the table, and you serve this delicious meal. We dine and dialogue together. What a thoroughly enjoyable evening!

Then, as I get up to leave, I reach into my pocket and say, "Now, what do I owe you?" You're *shocked*! That's an insult. You knew what I needed, and out of love for me, you fixed it and served it. Why, a major part of being a good host is that you pick up the tab. For me to suggest that I'll pay for it is like a slap in the face. You don't even want me to help with the dishes. Love motivated your giving me this great meal. It is your gift to me. To ask to pay for it repels your love.

Do you realize that there are men and women all around the world who are reaching in their pockets this very day and saying, "Okay, God . . . how much do I owe you?"

I have communicated this same message for years, but I will never forget the time I had a lady come to the platform after a meeting to see me. She had dissolved in tears. She said, "Here's my Bible. Would you sign your autograph in the back, just your autograph? And then," she added, "would you put underneath it in quotes 'Salvation is a *gift*'?"

"You see," she explained, "my background is religious, and all my life I've worked so hard. All my friends are from that same religious background, and they are still working so hard. Now — for the first time in my life, I realized that God is really offering me a gift. The thing I have noticed about all of us, all these years, is that not one of us has ever been secure. We've never known that salvation was ours *forever* — because we worked so hard for it. Our plan was to keep working so we could keep it in us."

She had been reaching into her purse all these years, trying to pay God for His gift. Was it free? No, not really. It cost Christ His life at the cross many centuries ago.

Third question: Is there any way to lose the gift? No, never! Now stop and think before you disagree. Stay with biblical logic, no human reasoning. If you work for it, then you can certainly lose it. And that would mean it's not a gift; it's what you've earned. We really confuse things when we try to turn a gift into a wage. Furthermore, just as no one can say how much work is enough to earn it, no one can say how little work is enough to lose it.

Salvation is simply a gift. It's simple, but it wasn't easy. It's free, but it wasn't cheap. It's yours, but it isn't automatic. You must receive it. When you do, it is yours forever.

TWO POSSIBLE RESPONSES

We're back to basics, Mr. Smith. When you return to the roots of salvation, you can either believe and accept this gift, or you can refuse and reject it. And you can go right on living, by the way. You won't suddenly get struck by lightning if you reject Christ. I've noticed that God doesn't immediately start doing bad things to people who refuse His Son. He doesn't make you look foolish. He won't suddenly cut your legs off at the knees. He doesn't scar your face or make you lose your job. He doesn't keep your car from starting because you reject the message. He doesn't kill your closest friend or cause your mate to leave you as a judgment because you didn't believe. That's not the way God operates.

He simply waits.

And that fakes people out. That makes some folks think that if He really meant it, then He'd zap them for refusing to take His gift. No. Not necessarily. Those who think like that don't understand God. He holds out His grace and He makes it available even if we choose to reject it.

ONE FINAL REMINDER

*B*ut I must remind you of something: You don't have forever. With no intention of manipulating you, you need to remember that death is certain. I wish I had kept track of the funeral services I have conducted in the last ten years on behalf of those who died before the age of fifty. Without trying to sound dramatic, I think it would shock you to know how many die before they turn fifty. And I'm sure some of them thought, "I've got a long time to go."

Listen, sin is terminal. And Mr. Smith, you've got that disease. It leads to death. It may not even be a year before you are gone . . . and you will have thought you had plenty of time.

I'm sure Peter Marshall thought he had a long, long time. May I return to his life? He was appointed to the Senate chaplaincy in early January 1947 . . . a specimen of good health. Yet it was just a shade beyond two years later when this forty-seven-year-old man was seized with a heart attack and died. He was as eloquent and creative as ever right up to the last . . . but within a matter of hours, his voice was hushed forever. Only the printed page speaks for Marshall today.

A sermon of his that one can never forget is what he called "The Tap on the Shoulder."

If you were walking down the street, and someone came up behind you and tapped you on the shoulder . . . what would you do? Naturally, you would turn around. Well, that is exactly what happens in the spiritual world. A man walks on through life—with the external call ringing in his ears, but with no response stirring in his heart, and then suddenly, without any warning, the Spirit taps him on the shoulder. The tap on the shoulder is the almighty power of God acting without help or hindrance . . . so as to produce a new creature, and to lead him into the particular work which God has for him.[6]

Maybe as you've read this chapter, you've felt God's tap on your shoulder. If so, respond. Stop reading. Close the book, bow your head, and tell the Lord you have felt His tap—and you want to accept His gift of eternal life. Thank Him for giving you His Son, Jesus Christ.

If you have done that, Mr. Smith . . . you have just met your Substitute.

Chapter 3

Gospel Basics — "Everyday Jesus"
by Greg Laurie

*C*an you think of someone whom you could never imagine as a Christian, someone so hardened, so resistant, and so far gone that he or she would never follow Jesus Christ? Or perhaps *you* are such a person. Or at least you like to think you are. Maybe you feel as though you wouldn't qualify to follow Jesus.

I was such a person. I was raised in a home plagued by divorce and alcoholism. "The OC" was my stomping ground. I went to school at Newport Harbor High in Newport Beach, California. I got into the party scene, drugs, and drinking, and then suddenly, I came to faith. I can tell you, it was the last thing I ever planned on doing, but thankfully, God had different plans than I did. My conversion was so unexpected that people didn't believe Greg Laurie had become a Christian. Yet when I look back on the decision I made and how some of my friends from those earlier days did not make it, I have no regrets whatsoever—not a single one.

Make no mistake about it: conversion is instantaneous. While the process of growing and maturing spiritually takes a lifetime, the actual work of conversion can take just seconds. This means that as you read this book, you can, quite literally, change within moments. You can leave this book different on the inside from when you began reading.

I want to briefly tell you the story of a man whose life was dramatically changed after one, seemingly short moment of contact with Jesus. He was a man who left his career, wealth, and power simply to become a follower of Jesus. It all happened when he came face-to-face with Jesus Christ, who said two words to him: "Follow Me."

His name was Matthew, and this is his story:

> As Jesus went on from there, He saw a man called Matthew, sitting in the tax collector's booth; and he said to him, "Follow Me!" And he got up and followed him. Then it happened that as Jesus was reclining at the table in the house, behold, many tax collectors and sinners came and were dining with Jesus and His disciples. When the Pharisees saw this, they said to His disciples, "Why is your Teacher eating with the tax collectors and sinners?" But when Jesus heard this, He said, "It is not those who are healthy who need a physician, but those who are sick." (Matthew 9:9–12)

I don't know about you, but there are two places I don't like to go: the doctor's office and the dentist's office. (I only go as a last resort, especially to the dentist.) It is probably because we're afraid of hearing some bad news. So somehow, we mistakenly believe that ignorance is bliss.

A man named Phil went to the doctor, and after a long checkup, his doctor said, "I have some bad news for you. You don't have long to live."

"How long do I have?" asked a distraught Phil.

"Ten," the doctor said sadly.

"Ten *what*? Months? Days?"

The doctor interrupted, "Nine, eight, seven . . . "

But back to our story. . . . Tax collectors were looked upon with great hatred by the Jews. For one thing, they collected taxes from their own fellow Jews for the Romans, who were the occupying power in Israel at the time. To make matters worse, tax collectors would often skim off the top or charge more than what was required, and then personally pocket the profit. It's very possible Matthew did that, but this was not the primary reason he was hated. He was considered a traitor, a turncoat, and a collaborator with Rome. Think of an ambulance-chasing lawyer, sleazy used-car salesman, and telemarketer all rolled into one, and you get the idea. Tax collectors barely ranked above plankton on the food chain. It would be like an American collecting intelligence for Al Qaeda. Matthew had aligned himself with the enemies of his own people. It's as though he had gone out of his way to offend his fellow Jews—and God.

We all know people who will do that. They will go far out of their way to offend, to upset, and to put off. Sometimes it is a cry for attention. And sometimes it is because they are running from what they know is right.

Are you running from God right now—perhaps going out of your way to offend Christians and anyone else? Perhaps you are under conviction, and that is why you do what you do. By conviction, I mean the Holy Spirit is making you more and more aware of your need for Jesus Christ, and you are fighting and resisting all the way. The ones who put up the biggest fight are often much closer to conversion than those who don't fight at all. As it's been said, "When you throw a rock into a pack of dogs, the one that barks the loudest is the one that was hit." Perhaps the reason you are "barking the loudest" or protesting the most is because you are closer to coming to Jesus than you like to let on.

But why had Matthew, also known as Levi, chosen this lifestyle that would alienate and offend so many? We don't know, but we do know this: he was most likely hated by all—all except Jesus, that is. Matthew's only "friends" would have been other tax collectors.

Maybe you feel as though you are hated. Maybe you are lonely, and you don't even know if you have any real friends to speak of. Maybe you hate the course your life has taken—perhaps you are into drugs, drinking, partying, or something else. You feel as though life has "chewed you up and spit you out." Or, maybe you have thought, *If only I could make the big bucks, then I will be happy.*

As hip-hop star Eminem once said in an interview, "You gotta be careful what you wish for. I always wished and hoped for this. But it's almost turning into more of a nightmare than a dream. I can't even go in public anymore. I've got the whole world looking at me! To be honest, I really have not had much support from family and friends. Just myself." [1]

Matthew was a very wealthy and successful man, but he was not happy either. He had turned his back on the very One who could help him: God. Perhaps something happened that turned him in this direction. Maybe he had been disillusioned by some rabbi or priest. Matthew had been raised to believe, but he turned away, or backslid.

It's amazing how many people will turn away from God at an early age because a minister, priest, or some person who claimed to be a Christian did not behave as one. People will turn away from

Jesus Christ today for the same reason (or excuse). In fact, there are two reasons people don't go to church:

1. They *don't* know a Christian.

2. They *do* know a Christian.

I personally want to apologize for all the Christians who have not been good representatives of Jesus Christ. But Jesus did not say to Matthew, "Follow My people." Rather, He said, "Follow Me." And He says that to you as well. I have been a follower of Jesus for well over thirty years, and I can tell you He has never been a hypocrite or inconsistent in any way. Sure, fellow Christians have disappointed me at times (and I'm sure I have disappointed some as well), but Jesus Christ has always been who He promised He was to me, and that is why I am following Him.

Matthew would have had a great seat at his strategically located tax booth. He may have even listened as Jesus taught from a boat. His heart, which undoubtedly had become hardened and bitter by the treatment of others, began to soften. But he couldn't bring himself to get up from that tax booth and go to Jesus. He probably was afraid Jesus would reject him: *Do I actually look so desperate that I would want a tax collector to follow Me?*

I used to be like that. I would hang out in Newport Beach, just wishing some Christian would talk to me, but they never really did. Thankfully, God could see past my hardened façade and called my name—just like He called Matthew's, and just like He is calling yours.

You may be thinking, *But I'm just not the religious type.* But God is not looking for the religious type. He is looking for the sinner type.

One day, Jesus saw Matthew and said two words that would forever change Matthew's life: "As Jesus went on from there, He saw a man called Matthew, sitting in the tax collector's booth; and He said to him, 'Follow Me!' And he got up and followed Him" (Matthew 9:9). The word *saw* in this verse is very suggestive. It means "to gaze intently upon, to stare, to fix one's eyes constantly upon an object." I'm sure that when people walked by Matthew, normally they would either turn away their eyes or look at him with scorn.

This word also means "to look right through." Have you ever had someone look right through you? Or, let me put it another way: do you have a mother? Jesus intentionally made eye contact with Matthew. And in the eyes of Jesus, Matthew saw many things: holiness and purity, to name a couple. But I'm certain he also saw love, compassion, and understanding. With their eyes fixed on each other, Jesus said two words that would reverberate through Matthew's soul, words that he never thought he would hear: "Follow Me." Jesus was choosing, selecting, and calling him out to be His disciple. And Jesus is saying the same thing to you right now.

But what does it mean to follow Jesus? Many claim to be His followers, but are we? As 2 Corinthians 13:5 reminds us, "Test yourselves to see if you are in the faith; examine yourselves! Or do you not recognize this about yourselves, that Jesus Christ is in you—unless indeed you fail the test?"

This phrase, "Follow Me," could also be translated, "Follow *with* Me," meaning companionship and friendship. Jesus was saying, "Matthew, I want you to be My friend!" Did you know that Jesus is saying the same to you right now? He wants you to bare your heart to Him, to tell Him your secrets, your fears, your hopes, and your dreams. Jesus said, "You are My friends if you do what I command you. No longer do I call you slaves, for the slave does not know what his master is doing; but I have called you friends, for all things that I have heard from My Father I have made known to you" (John 15:14–15).

Many people think God is out to ruin their lives. They believe He is always mad at them. Such was the case with a burglar who broke into a house one night. As he quietly made his way around, a voice suddenly spoke through the darkness: "I see you, and Jesus sees you too."

He stopped, amazed at what he had just heard. He waited for a few moments, and when nothing happened, he continued on.

For a second time the voice said, "I see you, and Jesus sees you too."

Stunned, the burglar turned on his flashlight for a look around the room. To his surprise and relief, he saw a large birdcage in the corner with a parrot inside.

"Did you say that?" he asked the parrot.

"I see you, and Jesus sees you too," the parrot repeated for the third time.

"Why, it's a parrot!" laughed the burglar. But then the burglar saw a large Doberman with its teeth bared, looking at him.

The parrot then said to the Doberman, "Sic 'em, Jesus!"

That's how a lot of people see Jesus: ready to pounce on them and ruin their lives. Nothing could be further from the truth. The fact is, God loves you, and His plan for you is good. God says, "For I know the plans that I have for you . . . plans for welfare and not for calamity, to give you a future and a hope" (Jeremiah 29:11).

Jesus told the story of a prodigal son who demanded his inheritance from his father and then left home and ended up wasting it all on immoral living. When he came to his senses and realized that even his father's servants had it better than he did, he decided to go home. His father, who spotted him coming down the road one day, ran out to meet him and threw his arms around him. He welcomed him home and even threw him a party. This father was overjoyed that his prodigal son had come home.

In the same way, when we have sinned against God, He misses us, just as that father missed his wayward son. God wants to be your friend. The question is, do you want to be His? There are a lot of people running around today who claim to be friends of Jesus. But if you are a true friend of Jesus, then you will obey Him. Remember, Jesus said, "You are My friends if you do what I *command* you" (John 15:14, emphasis added). It is not for us to pick and choose which parts of the Bible we like and then throw out the rest. What God offers is a package deal.

When Jesus said to Matthew, "Follow Me," the word *follow* that He used comes from a Greek word meaning "to walk the same road." It is in the imperative, meaning that Jesus's statement was not only an invitation, but also a command. The word is also a verb in the present tense, commanding the beginning of an action and continuing habitually in it. In other words, Jesus was essentially saying, "I command you to follow Me each and every day."

Following Jesus is not something we do only on Sunday. He is not "Sunday Jesus," but "everyday Jesus." He wants to go with you to church, to school, to work, to the movies, as you surf the Net, and wherever you go.

The Bible tells us that Matthew "got up and followed Him" (Matthew 9:9). Luke's Gospel adds this detail: "And he [Matthew]

left everything behind, and got up and began to follow Him"
(Luke 5:28).

Matthew, recognizing the immense privilege being offered,
without hesitation, stood up and followed Jesus. Do you realize what
a privilege it is that Jesus is calling you? As I already mentioned, He
called me more than three decades ago as a confused and angry kid.
I wonder where I would be today if I hadn't followed Him.

You may wonder, *If I follow Jesus, will I have to give up anything?*
You will give up emptiness, loneliness, guilt, and the fear of death.
In its place, Jesus will give you fulfillment, friendship, forgiveness,
and the guarantee of heaven when you die. It is God's "trade-in
deal," and it is here for you right now.

It would be like hearing a knock at your front door at home.

"Who is it?" you call out.

"It's Jesus!" a voice replies. "I stand at the door and knock, and if
you will hear My voice and open the door, I will come in!"

You quickly open the door, and there He stands: Jesus Christ.
You quickly invite Him in to your front room.

Nervously you ask, "Could I get you something to eat, Jesus?"

"Of course. Thank you," He answers.

You rush into your kitchen, open the door to the refrigerator,
and all that is there is day-old pizza and a few deviled eggs. Somehow these do not seem appropriate. As you are thinking about what
to give Jesus to eat, you hear a lot of noise coming from the front
room, so you run back in, and there stands Jesus, taking down your
pictures from the wall. In the short time you were out of the room,
He has already thrown all your furniture onto the front lawn.

Now He is proceeding to tear up your carpet, so you cry out, "Jesus, with all due respect, what are You doing?"

"A little spring cleaning," He calmly responds.

"But Jesus, this is all my stuff here, and frankly, if I would have known you were going to get rid of it, I might not have let You in to begin with!"

He ignores your outburst and gives a loud whistle as He gestures to the large moving truck backing up to your driveway. Emblazoned on the sides of it are the words, *Father and Son Moving Company*.

"Bring it in, boys!" Jesus smiles.

Two very large men lay down the most beautiful carpet you have ever seen. Then they begin to put up a color-coordinated, lush wall covering. Then, new hand-done works of art are hung in the place of your old ones.

"You have really good taste, Jesus!"

"Yes, I do. Don't forget, I did create the heavens and the earth," He answers.

"Good point there, Lord!" you sheepishly respond.

Then gorgeous, hand-crafted furniture is carefully laid on your new carpet, and suddenly it dawns on you: Jesus only took away the old things to put something better in their place.

When a person really meets Jesus Christ, he or she cannot leave the old life fast enough. Old habits, standards, and practices are no longer appealing and are gladly left behind. But far from being depressed about what he left behind, Matthew's heart overflowed with joy. He lost a career, but gained a destiny. He lost his material possessions, but gained a spiritual fortune. He lost his temporary security, but gained eternal life. He gave up all this world had to offer, but found Jesus.

You may be like Matthew. Maybe you don't have many friends. Maybe you feel alone and empty. Jesus is looking at you right now and saying, "Follow Me!"

He offers you the forgiveness of sin, the hope of heaven, and peace instead of turmoil. He offers you friendship and companionship instead of loneliness. He offers you heaven instead of hell. But you must come to Him—not tomorrow, not next week, month, or year, but now. Jesus is saying to you right now, "Follow Me!"

You may think, *God could never change someone like me!* But He can—and will—right now. The Bible says, "Therefore, if anyone is in Christ, he is a new creature; the old things passed away; behold, new things have come" (2 Corinthians 5:17). Would you like a fresh start? A new beginning? Would you like to never be alone again?

Or have you, like Matthew, fallen away from the faith? You can come back to Christ today.

So, what do you need to do to be a true follower of Jesus?

First, realize that you are a sinner. The Bible teaches that, "All have sinned and fall short of the glory of God" (Romans 3:23). That means no more excuses. Stop blaming your parents, your addictive behavior, your dog, or your cat. Like the tax collector in Luke's Gospel, you need to say, "God, be merciful to me, the sinner!" (Luke 18:13).

Second, recognize that Jesus died on the cross for you. Jesus said, "Greater love has no one than this, that one lay down his life for his friends" (John 15:13). Jesus willingly died for our sin.

Third, repent of your sin. The Bible says, "God is now declaring to men that all people everywhere should repent" (Acts 17:30). This is missing in the so-called conversions of many people. Turn from all known sin.

Fourth, receive Christ into your life. It is not enough to just believe He is the Son of God; it is also receiving Him into your life. Jesus said, "Behold, I stand at the door and knock; if anyone hears My voice and opens the door, I will come in to him and will dine with him, and he with Me" (Revelation 3:20). And the Bible promises, "But as many as received Him, to them He gave the right to become children of God, even to those who believe in His name" (John 1:12).

Fifth, do it now. The Bible says, "Behold, now is 'the acceptable time,' behold, now is 'the day of salvation'" (2 Corinthians 6:2). Matthew made a public stand for Jesus Christ. He got right up from that tax booth and followed Jesus.

It would seem to me that Matthew was more of a backslider than an unbeliever. He was raised in the way of the Lord. He knew the Bible, but rebelled. But when Jesus spoke to Him, He followed.

Have you fallen away from the Lord? Are you living in such a way that if Christ were to return, you wouldn't be ready? God says, "Return, you backsliding children, and I will heal your backslidings" (Jeremiah 3:22 NKJV).

Chapter 4

Evangelism Tools

Harvest Ministries and Insight for Living

"Whoever will call on the name of the Lord will be saved." How then will they call on Him in whom they have not believed? How will they believe in Him whom they have not heard? And how will they hear without a preacher? How will they preach unless they are sent? Just as it is written, "How beautiful are the feet of those who bring good news of good things!" (Romans 10:13–15).

In this passage, the apostle Paul lists some excellent questions about the obstacles unbelievers face before coming to belief in Christ. They must believe. But in order to believe, they must hear. And in order to hear, someone must be willing to speak. And that someone must share the good news.

This section contains some helpful tools to assist believers in sharing the good news with others. Harvest Ministries offers some common reasons believers don't share the gospel and then presents some good motivation to begin doing so. Harvest then provides guidelines for creating a simple, one-minute testimony that any believer can adapt in order to share his or her own personal story with others. Next, Insight for Living offers a simple, evangelistic diagram that illustrates a believer's need to accept Christ. A short question-and-answer session follows, presenting helpful insights into issues of faith and spiritual growth.

❧

Common Reasons We Don't Share the Gospel
Harvest Ministries

We Don't Care

Why are so many of us reluctant to share the gospel? The reason many of us rarely share is because we do not want to. And the reason we do not want to is because (if we are completely honest) we do not care.

We hear so much about the need for evangelism. We hear sermons on how to do it and see programs designed to mobilize the church in this area. Yet, all this is of no consequence if we are lacking one basic element: a burden and concern for the lost.

Four primary reasons should cause us to care about sharing the gospel. First, we are grateful for what God has done for us, and we want to give something back to Him as a form of spiritual worship. This natural response has been placed in our hearts by the Spirit of God. The primary job of the Holy Spirit is to point to Jesus, lifting Him up so that all people will come to Him.

Second, we should not share the gospel with others out of obligation, duty, or guilt, but out of a God-given burden for their lives. The apostle Paul showed this compassion, writing "I have great sorrow and unceasing grief in my heart. For I could wish that I myself were accursed from Christ for my brethren, my countrymen according to the flesh" (Romans 9:2–3 NKJV). Paul cared for his kinsmen so much that he was willing to go to hell (if necessary) so that others could go to heaven. No wonder he had such a powerful and effective ministry!

If you ask the Lord to stir your heart and to give you a burden for those who are like sheep without a shepherd, you will not be disappointed. He may call you to cross the sea as a missionary — or perhaps to just cross the street!

Third, God uses evangelism to grow us and prepare us for eternity. Remember, we are not doing God a favor by sharing the gospel with others. He does not need us to do His work. He has many other means at His disposal. He has *chosen* to use us in this way, because as we participate with Him, we grow spiritually. His chief aim for His children is to prepare us for eternity. And we are prepared as we obediently follow Him. If we do not follow Jesus in this way, we cannot fully mature as believers.

Finally, God has prepared a special crown in heaven for those who lead others to Him. It is not wrong to be motivated by heavenly reward. If it were, why would God promise it to us as an incentive for service? England's Queen Victoria once said that she hoped Jesus would return in her lifetime so that she could lay her crown at His feet. Wouldn't it be wonderful to have many crowns to throw at the feet of Jesus when He returns for His church?

We Don't Know Enough

Many people complain they don't know enough to share the gospel. They claim they don't know enough Scripture verses or the right words to lead someone in the sinner's prayer. They think it would be better to let their pastor or an evangelist share the gospel. After all, it is their job to preach the gospel, right?

While it is true that a pastor's job and an evangelist's job are to preach the gospel, it is also every Christian's responsibility.

Second Timothy 4:5 tells us to "do the work of an evangelist." This means that it is our duty to learn what we do not know. More importantly, it is our duty to share our personal testimonies, which requires very little Bible knowledge.

Sharing the gospel is just like one beggar showing another beggar where he or she found bread.

Your own story of how you came to faith in Christ is a story worth telling. The wonderful thing about your testimony is that even if you are a relatively new Christian, you can still share about what God has done for you personally. Consider the blind man whom Jesus miraculously healed. As the religious authorities cross-examined the blind man on the finer points of theology, he gave this classic response: "One thing I do know, that though I was blind, now I see" (John 9:25). You, too, have a similar story of how Jesus healed you of your sin. This is a story you should always be ready to share.

Caution! Never substitute your testimony for the gospel. Always use your story to illustrate the power of the gospel!

We Don't Know Any Non-Christians

Many Christians claim they can't share the gospel because everyone they know is a Christian. Though this may seem hard to believe, it is a symptom of a greater problem. If you don't know any non-Christians, you are not going into the world and preaching the gospel (Mark 16:15). You do not have spiritual eyes to see those God has placed all around you. One famous salesman has said that we all know at least 250 people whom we influence to make decisions in one way or another. Ask God to open your eyes to see the great harvest before you (John 4:35).

In order to share the gospel and to be the salt of the earth, we need to make contact with those who do not know Christ. The world is not supposed to go into the church; the church is supposed to go into the world. If you don't know anyone who is a non-Christian, you need to make the effort to meet some new people. After all, Christ commanded this; He did not recommend it.

We Are Afraid to Fail

According to a study done among believers, fear of failure is the number-one reason people do not attempt to share Christ with their friends. This fear comes from an improper understanding of our responsibility before the Lord. We cannot convert anyone, nor should we try. Conversion is the work of the Holy Spirit. However, our words are an essential link in the process of unleashing the power of the gospel into an individual's life.

Don't overestimate your role or responsibility in the conversion process. Either mistake can become a roadblock to this step of obedience in your spiritual life.

One-Minute Message
Harvest Ministries

> "One thing I do know, that though I was blind, now I
> see." (John 9:25)

*Y*our personal testimony is a resource to help you build bridges,
instead of burning them, when you share the gospel with others.
It allows people to see that you were once in their shoes but have
now been transformed by the power of Christ. To help you share
your testimony, Harvest Ministries has developed the *One-Minute
Message*. This handy reference will help you share the gospel through
the story of what God has done in your life.

Three Keys of a One-Minute Message

1. My Life before Christ

Don't glorify your past, but mention what your life was like before
Christ.

> "I had a void in my life that nothing could fill."
> (Ecclesiastes 3:11)
>
> "I felt separated from God." (Isaiah 59:2)
>
> "My life was dominated by sin and with pleasing
> myself." (Luke 15:11–24)

Share how you never felt that you could become the person you
ought to be.

2. My Life Changed by Christ

Now summarize how you came into a relationship with Christ.

Be sure to mention the key elements of the gospel:

"I *realized* that I'm a sinner and that I fall short of God's glory." (Romans 3:23)

"I *recognized* that Christ died on the cross for my sins." (Romans 5:8)

"I *repented* or turned away from my sins." (Acts 3:19)

"I *received* Christ as Lord of my life." (Revelation 3:20)

3. My New Life in Christ

Talk about how your life is noticeably different now that you are in Christ.

Put into your own words the following benefits of being in Christ:

"I now have peace in my life" (Romans 5:1).

"Now that I'm a Christian, I know I have a purpose for living." (Jeremiah 29:11)

"I now have the assurance that I'm going to heaven." (John 3:36).

Draw Me a Picture
Insight for Living

⍟ne of the most powerful tools you can use to explain the gospel is a simple diagram. You can sketch it anywhere—on a napkin at a restaurant, in the sand at the beach, or on the back of a business card. Take a few moments to study it, and be sure to look up the verses and slip them into your memory.

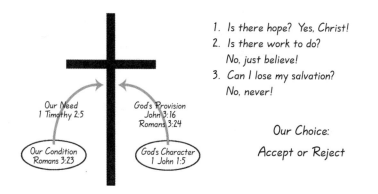

Do you think you can talk your way through this diagram? Try following this procedure:

On a separate piece of paper, begin by sketching the circle on the left and writing, "Our Condition, Romans 3:23." Review this verse, and summarize it in your own words.

Next, draw the other circle, and write, "God's Character, 1 John 1:5." Again, summarize this verse as simply as you can. To help the person visualize the barrier between us and God, draw the vertical line of the cross between the two circles.

Sketch the arrow that goes from left to right, and write, "Our Need, 1 Timothy 2:5." Using this verse, describe its meaning in one sentence.

Finally, pencil in the arrow that goes from right to left, and finish the cross by drawing the horizontal line. Write, "God's Provision, John 3:16; Romans 3:24." Review these verses, and restate them in your own words.

After you finish explaining what Christ has accomplished for us on the cross, write down the three questions, answering them one at a time. Conclude by writing, "Our Choice: Accept or Reject." Your purpose is not to manipulate a decision, but simply to lay out the fact that the gospel requires a response. Either we believe it or we don't.

Some people may not be ready to accept Christ, and yet they may not be willing to reject Him either. God never forces His grace on anyone, and neither should we. However, we can help the person see that choosing not to accept Him is really the same as rejecting Him. There is no middle ground.

If the person needs time to think, give him plenty of room. Before concluding your time together, perhaps ask him if he can pinpoint what issue or question is holding him back. Sometimes talking about it will help him resolve it. You may also wish to put into his hands one of these books: *Who Is This Jesus?* by Michael Green (Nashville: Thomas Nelson Publishers, 1992) or *Reason to Believe: A Response to Common Objections to Christianity* by R. C. Sproul (Grand Rapids: Zondervan, 1982).

If the person is ready to accept Christ, that's wonderful! You may encourage your friend to express his decision to the Lord in prayer. There's no magic formula for this prayer. The thief on the cross simply cried out, "Jesus, remember me when You come into Your kingdom!" (Luke 23:42). If your friend needs help, you may use the following prayer as a guide:

Dear God,

I know that my sin has put a barrier between You and me. Thank You for sending Jesus to die in my place. I accept Your gift of eternal life and ask Jesus to be my personal Savior. Please begin to guide my life. Thank You. In Jesus's name, amen.

Never underestimate the power of the gospel. It can change a person's life — forever.

⁂

Common Questions: Dealing with Issues of Faith and Spiritual Growth
Insight for Living

Q: Why should I believe the Bible? How do I know that it's true?

A: We believe the Bible because it's God's inspired Word, it claims to be true, and it proves itself to be true in the lives of believers. Paul wrote in 1 Thessalonians 2:13:

> For this reason we also constantly thank God that when you received the word of God which you heard from us, you accepted it not as the word of men, but for what it really is, the word of God, which also performs its work in you who believe.

The prophet Isaiah calls God "the God of truth" in Isaiah 65:16. Our Father reveals His truth to us primarily through the Bible. In Matthew 4:4, Jesus attested to the truth and authority of Scripture when He said, "Man shall not live on bread alone, but on every word that proceeds out of the mouth of God." The psalmist also testified to the veracity of Scripture:

You are near, O Lord,

And all Your commandments are truth. (Psalm 119:151)

The sum of Your word is truth,

And every one of Your righteous ordinances is

everlasting. (Psalm 119:160)

God has no intention of hiding His perfect truth from the people He so lovingly created. He desires for every person on earth to come to a knowledge of the truth (1 Timothy 2:4), so He reveals His truth to us through His Word. The fact that He is truth guarantees that He will reveal Himself as He really is, that His revelation will be perfectly reliable, that what He says will correspond exactly to the way things are. At least four times in Scripture, we're assured that God does not lie (Numbers 23:19; 1 Samuel 15:29; Titus 1:2; and Hebrews 6:18). When the Almighty speaks, His words are true and accurate.

Q: I understand that Jesus Christ is much more than just a "great moral teacher," but how do I know that He's the true Messiah prophesied about in Scripture?

A: We can look back at Old Testament prophecies and discern two distinct lines of prophecy regarding the coming of the Messiah. One line predicted the first coming of the Messiah as the suffering Savior who would redeem His people by dying on the cross and then rising from the dead (Psalm 22; Isaiah 52:13–53:12). The other line of prophecy foretold the eternal kingdom that the Messiah would establish after He had atoned for the sins of His people (Isaiah 9:6–7; Daniel 7:13–14).

These two prophecies concerning the Messiah were not fully understood by the Old Testament saints, but we understand them now because of the testimonies of the gospel writers and the explanation of prophecies by the apostle Paul. When the Lord Jesus Christ presented Himself to the nation of Israel, He did so as their promised Messiah. In Luke chapter 4, He presented Himself as the fulfillment of Isaiah's prophecy (Isaiah 61:1–2). By His works, Jesus validated His power and authority to make such a claim. By His teaching, He revealed the true nature of His Messiahship and His eternal kingdom.

However, most Israelites had a different kind of Messiah in mind. They sought a Messiah of earthly magnificence, awesome power, and military might rather than one of humility who emptied Himself of glory to come to earth, take on human flesh, and die to save us from our sins (Philippians 2:5–8). Consequently, some people began to withdraw from Christ, and the Jewish leadership in His day quickly began to resist Him as a threat to their concept of who the Messiah "should be."

None of this caught Christ by surprise. He knew that He must first suffer before He could reign. Jesus began to withdraw from ministry to the masses and to pour His life into His disciples. He began to teach the crowds in the mysterious, veiled language of parables. He spoke less about His earthly kingdom and more about His plan for the church. He dealt less with Jews and more with Gentiles. He rebuked the Jewish leaders more openly, revealing their error. He even willingly submitted to the Father's plan and accepted death by the hands of His opponents—just as the Scriptures predicted the Messiah would do.

The Bible records and supports the authentication of Jesus Christ as Israel's Messiah, as well as His presentation of Himself as the Son of God and His rejection by His own people. All of these events fulfill the Old Testament prophecies concerning the Messiah and confirm that Jesus truly was the long-awaited One referred to in the Old Testament Scriptures.

Q: Is Jesus the only way to God? If so, how do we know?

A: Many passages of Scripture confirm that God has made salvation available to us by faith alone — faith in the birth, death, and resurrection of His Son, Jesus Christ, and the eternal, abundant life that He offers us. Probably the best-known passage supporting this truth is John 14:6, where Jesus says to Thomas, "I am the way, and the truth, and the life; no one comes to the Father but through Me." Other supporting passages are:

> God has given us eternal life, and this life is in His Son. He who has the Son has the life; he who does not have the Son of God does not have the life. (1 John 5:11–12)

> He [Jesus] is the stone which was rejected by you, the builders, but which became the chief corner stone. And there is salvation in no one else; for there is no other name under heaven that has been given among men by which we must be saved. (Acts 4:11–12)

> If you confess with your mouth Jesus as Lord, and believe in your heart that God raised Him from the dead, you will be saved; for with the heart a person believes, resulting in righteousness, and with the mouth he confesses, resulting in salvation. (Romans 10:9–10)

Christ came to earth, died, and rose again to offer us salvation. We believe God's Word to be true, and we experience the truth of Scripture's words, its claims, and its principles in our daily lives. Scripture claims that Christ is the only way to salvation;

God claims that Christ is the only way; Jesus Himself claims in no uncertain terms that He is the only way; and the apostles and saints have affirmed throughout history that Jesus is the only way. If these claims are true, then the contradictory claims of other religions and philosophies that *they* are the only way (or alternative ways) to reach the same goal must be false. Jesus Himself taught that "the gate is small and the way is narrow that leads to life, and there are few who find it" (Matthew 7:14).

Christ is the only doorway to salvation, but the door's wide open! God wants every person to come to Him in faith, claiming redemption through Christ. The apostle Peter wrote in 2 Peter 3:9, "The Lord is not slow about His promise, as some count slowness, but is patient toward you, not wishing for any to perish but for all to come to repentance." Once we have chosen to walk through the door of salvation, we have the privilege of graciously sharing our message with others who may not realize or understand that Christ is the *only* way to God.

Q: I recently attended a church where the pastor taught that a person must be baptized by immersion before he or she can be truly saved. Is this true? What does the Bible say?

A: If we say that a person has to be baptized to be saved, we are adding something to the *only* prerequisite the Bible requires of a person for salvation: *faith*. The apostle Paul used Abraham as the leading example of one who was saved by grace through faith alone—before the rite of circumcision, before the Old Testament Law (Romans 4:9–13).

More specifically, the New Testament teaches the ordinance of "believer's baptism." One who has believed in Christ may be baptized to signify his or her faith (Acts 10:47; 11:17; 19:1–5).

In every biblical context where water baptism is mentioned along with belief, faith always precedes the ordinance (1 Peter 3:21).

In biblical contexts where baptism is included in the proclamation of the gospel, the inclusion of the ordinance of baptism only indicates a public transfer of allegiance to Christ. For example, Peter's command in Acts 2:38, "be baptized in the name of Jesus Christ for the forgiveness of your sins," is often misapplied in the church today. Peter gave the sermon in a context of Jews who would have understood baptism as a *proof* of faith—not a *part* of faith. Most of us in America have no qualms about being baptized in public. But in many other countries today, the meaning of water baptism is much more similar to what it was in Acts 2—a testimony to the community and to the world. It represents a complete break from the past. And it is common for newly baptized Christians to be arrested, spend time in jail, lose their family—or even lose their lives for the sake of the gospel.

Q: Why do so many unbelievers experience health, wealth, success, and happiness when they're not honoring God? Is God rewarding them?

A: King Solomon concluded that life apart from God is boring, empty, profitless, and purposeless. Yet all of us have encountered unbelievers and even atheists who appear to experience happiness and excitement in life. Does that contradict Solomon's conclusions?

The truth is that unbelievers and the ungodly will experience temporary enjoyment in life, even apart from a saving relationship with Christ. This is due to the gift of *common grace*, defined as "grace that is available to all humanity. Its benefits are experienced by all human beings without discrimination. It reaches out in a multitude of ways, promoting what is good and restraining what is evil."[1] Our loving Heavenly Father extends a certain grace even to those who reject Him and His gift of eternal life through His Son. Several forms of common grace include the revelation of God through nature (Romans 1:18–20), His provision of sunshine, rain, and crops in due season (Acts 14:16–17), ordered human government (Romans 13:1–2), and the presence of truth and beauty in the world (Philippians 4:8).[2]

Though unbelievers may experience some blessing and joy in the present, justice and wrath are stored up for them in eternity. In contrast, while believers experience the common effects of a sinful world now, in the world to come they will receive the full blessings of salvation.

Q: When I trust Christ, what can I expect will happen? Will I be the same or different? How will I know?

A: When we make the crucial decision to trust Jesus Christ as our Savior, two vital changes take place.

First of all, something happens deep *within* us. According to 2 Corinthians 5:17, we become an entirely new creation. We gain new motivations and new interests. Our interests began to shift from ourselves to others—from the things of the flesh to the things of God. And a new group of people appears on the horizon of our lives—other Christians. We begin to be more vulnerable, more open, and more willing to confess our sin. Our desire to hide from God changes to a desire to spend more time with Him. Why? We become new creatures within.

Second, something happens *to* us. When we express our faith in Christ, we instantaneously enter the family of God. We may not feel any different at that exact moment, but something vital happens the moment we believe. We become a part of God's family forever.

When we choose to trust God, we become new creatures, and we join God's family. And those two things never change!

Q: I'm confused about the "sin nature" that I often hear other Christians talking about. After I became a Christian, did I lose my sin nature? If not, then what separates me as a believer from non-Christians?

A: The marvelous working of God in the life of a believer begins at the point of faith in Christ. The Bible speaks of a believer's life before Christ as the "old man," while the "new man" represents a Christian's spiritual rebirth. However, the apostle Paul's teaching that the "old man was crucified" with Christ (Romans 6:6) and yet still exists as something that we as believers must choose to "lay aside" (Ephesians 4:22) has led to some misunderstanding about what we call our "old nature" and our "new nature."

This confusion stems, in part, from a vague understanding of the term *nature*. The expression never refers specifically to a person or thing, but to the *qualities* or *characteristics* of a person or thing. For example, Jesus has two natures—human and divine—eternally joined in one person. While He lived on earth, Christ expressed both His humanity and divinity as one man. His dual natures existed in perfect harmony. Our "sinful nature" and our "saintly nature," on the other hand, do not.

From one perspective, we have two natures because the attributes of both sin and righteousness remain within us, and these two natures are at war with one another (Romans 7:15–25). But from another perspective, God sees us with all "old things passed away" (2 Corinthians 5:17)—as people who now have righteous standing through the death and resurrection of Christ. Because

Scripture teaches aspects of both perspectives, we cannot make them mutually exclusive.

Christ has "done away with" (or literally, "made powerless") our sinful nature (Romans 6:6). This doesn't mean the sinful nature no longer exists, but it *no longer has the power to make us sin.* The fact that Christians now find their identity in Christ alone does not mean the old, sinful nature no longer exerts its influence on us. It only means we don't have to respond to it because we have the power of the Holy Spirit to help us overcome the temptation to sin.

Q: I've prayed over and over again for God to take away a particular sin in my life, but I keep falling into the same sin. Does this mean that my heart hasn't truly been changed?

A: While we as believers will still commit some sins after we accept Christ, our lives should not be carnal or controlled by negative sin patterns. We're no longer in bondage to sin or our fleshly desires. God has granted us the ability to exercise wisdom, discernment, self-control, and discipline as the Holy Spirit guides our thoughts, words, and actions.

Knowing Scripture, being accountable to others, and practicing daily spiritual disciplines are some of the best ways to arm yourself against dangerous sin patterns. The daily practice of the spiritual life is part of the means by which believers are able to more intimately know their God, relate to and rest in their new life in Christ, and experience true spiritual change and liberation from life-dominating patterns of sin. The spiritual disciplines promote growth in our devotion to God and our ability to grasp, personalize, believe, and apply Scripture to our lives.

Assembling together weekly with other believers for accountability, fellowship, worship, ministry, prayer, and the teaching of

God's Word is also vital to our spiritual health. The Holy Spirit does not operate in a mindless vacuum devoid of God's point of view. The Word and the Spirit work together, so that if we fail to take time to get alone with God and His Word two things will happen: we will quench the ministry of the Spirit, and we will be influenced and deceived by the negative attitudes and ungodly viewpoints of the world around us.

Our heavenly Father may allow *trials* in our lives, but He will never *tempt* us to sin. James wrote:

> Let no one say when he is tempted, "I am being tempted by God"; for God cannot be tempted by evil, and He Himself does not tempt anyone. But each one is tempted when he is carried away and enticed by his own lust. Then when lust has conceived, it gives birth to sin; and when sin is accomplished, it brings forth death. (James 1:13–15)

See the progression? Sin and temptation are part of an insidious process by which our fleshly lusts and desires lead to sin, and our sin, ultimately, leads to spiritual death. But God's power triumphs over both Satan's power and the power of our own desires. God's Word promises us that,

> No temptation has overtaken you but such as is common to man; and God is faithful, who will not allow you to be tempted beyond what you are able, but with the temptation will provide the way of escape also, so that you will be able to endure it." (1 Corinthians 10:13)

Paul wrote, "If anyone is in Christ, he is a new creature; the old things passed away; behold, new things have come" (2 Corinthians 5:17). When we look at the delicate finery of a butterfly's wings, we find it hard to believe that this exquisite creature was once a fat, ugly caterpillar crawling around in the dirt. You've experienced spiritual metamorphosis; you're a new creature. Are you living like it?

Q: Is it possible to do something that would cause me to lose my salvation?

A: Romans 8:38–39 says that no "created thing" can separate us from the love of God, given to us through Jesus Christ. Because you and I are "created thing[s]," Paul states very strongly that under no circumstance could we ever do something that would cause us to lose our salvation.

Earlier in the same chapter of Romans, Paul says that "those whom [God] justified, He also glorified" (8:30). From our perspective, we have not yet been glorified; that will not happen in this life. But from God's perspective, it's already done. Our salvation is complete in His sight, including the initial moment of salvation called *justification*, the ongoing work of salvation called *sanctification*, and the final work of salvation called *glorification*. What greater assurance do we need that God would not under any circumstance undo the work which He has already completed? Jesus affirmed this truth in John 10:27–28: "My sheep hear My voice, and I know them, and they follow Me; and I give eternal life to them, and they will never perish; and no one will snatch them out of My hand."

Chapter 5

Recommended Resources

Harvest Ministries

Harvest Ministries. *How to Follow Jesus*. Riverside, Calif.: Harvest, 2005.

Harvest Ministries. *Impact: Equipping Believers to Impact Their World*. Riverside, Calif.: Harvest, 2003.

Harvest Ministries. *One-Minute Message Card*. Riverside, Calif.: Harvest, 2003.

Laurie, Greg. *Dealing with Giants: How to Face the Hardships and Challenges of Life*. Dana Point, Calif.: Kerygma, 2005.

Laurie, Greg. *How to Know God: Crusade Messages 2004–2005*. Dana Point, Calif.: Kerygma, 2006.

Laurie, Greg, ed. *New Believer's Bible*. Wheaton, Ill.: Tyndale House, 1996.

Laurie, Greg. *New Believer's Guide to How to Share Your Faith*. Wheaton, Ill.: Tyndale House, 1999.

Laurie, Greg. *Strengthening Your Faith: Messages from the Gospel of John*. Dana Point, Calif.: Kerygma, 2005.

Laurie, Greg. *Strengthening Your Marriage* (DVD). Riverside, Calif.: Harvest, 2006.

Insight for Living

Swindoll, Charles R. *The Grace Awakening*. Nashville: W Publishing Group, 2003.

Swindoll, Charles R. *Growing Deep in the Christian Life: Essential Truths for Becoming Strong in the Faith*. Grand Rapids: Zondervan, 1995.

Swindoll, Charles R. *Perfect Trust*. Nashville: J. Countryman, 2000.

Swindoll, Charles R. *So, You Want to Be Like Christ? Eight Essentials to Get You There*. Nashville: W Publishing Group, 2005.

Swindoll, Charles R. *So, You Want to Be Like Christ? Eight Essentials to Get You There Workbook*. Nashville: W Publishing Group, 2005.

Swindoll, Charles R. *Start Where You Are: Catch a Fresh Vision for Your Life*. Nashville: W Publishing Group, 1999.

Swindoll, Charles R. *Strengthening Your Grip: How to Live Confidently in an Aimless World*. Nashville: W Publishing Group, 1998.

Insight for Living

Insight for Living is the Bible-teaching radio ministry of Charles R. Swindoll. Since 1979, Chuck's practical, biblical messages have been aired and distributed all over the world. Our thirty-minute, daily radio broadcast, *Insight for Living*, now airs worldwide on more than two thousand radio outlets and is currently heard in seven languages on six continents—North America, South America, Australia, Asia, Africa, and Europe.

Through its international ministries, Insight for Living is making the gospel available to spiritually hungry people throughout the world in languages and expressions they can easily understand. Theologically-trained field pastors who are passionately serving in their own cultures adapt the broadcasts of *Insight for Living* in ways that impact their audiences with the profound and practical messages that English-language listeners have cherished for over twenty-five years.

In addition to the daily broadcast, Insight for Living offers many quality resources to aid people in their study of the Bible as they seek to deepen their relationships with Jesus Christ. Available resources include more than two thousand sermons, as well as Bible Companions, LifeMaps, journals, children's resources, booklets, and more. Insight for Living's monthly newsletter, *Insights*, is specially designed to encourage listeners in their personal, spiritual growth.

Insight for Living's Web site, www.insight.org, offers podcasts—conveniently allowing listeners to download Chuck's messages onto iPods® or other MP3 players. In the *Beyond the Broadcast* section of the site, a wealth of additional resources is provided to supplement each sermon series heard on the radio. The Web site also presents many topical and expositional articles containing biblical teaching and practical insight from seminary-trained pastors, theologians, and counselors.

Chuck Swindoll and Insight for Living are committed to excellence in communicating the truths of Scripture and the Person of Jesus Christ in an accurate, clear, and practical manner so that people will come to an understanding of God's plan for their lives, as well as their significant role as authentic Christians in a needy, hostile, and desperate world.

Harvest Outreach Ministries

Harvest Outreach Ministries is the ministry of Greg Laurie, senior pastor of Harvest Christian Fellowship in Riverside, California. Whether through the local church, radio, Internet, television, or Harvest Crusades, Pastor Greg and Harvest are committed to their mission of knowing God and making Him known.

A New Beginning with Greg Laurie, the internationally syndicated radio program, is heard every day in more than five hundred communities around the U.S. and by more than three million people overseas. More than eight thousand listeners accept Christ as Lord and Savior every year.

Harvest Online, Pastor Greg's Web outreach at www.harvest.org, provides a large collection of resources that help people experience a deeper relationship with God through daily devotions, live webcasts, television and radio archives, and much more. And Harvest Online's podcasts allow the flexibility of automatically receiving audio and video programs featuring Greg Laurie's relevant and biblical messages on an iPod or MP3 player.

Pastor Greg's television program, *Knowing God with Greg Laurie*, features his down-to-earth, straightforward Bible teaching, supported by testimonies from real people who have been radically changed by Christ. Nominated in 2005 for the Annual Media Award for Best Television Teaching Program, *Knowing God with Greg Laurie* is seen on more than twenty-five television outlets throughout the U.S. and in other countries, such as Australia and New Zealand.

Since 1990, Harvest Ministries has been making God known through its contemporary, large-scale, evangelistic outreaches called Harvest Crusades. Organized nationally and internationally by local churches, more than three million people have attended Harvest Crusades, with well over a quarter of a million people making decisions to follow Christ.

Whether on the radio, television, online, or in the local church, Pastor Greg Laurie and Harvest Ministries apply biblical principles to current events in a way that is relevant and easily understood by people of all ages from all walks of life.

Endnotes

Chapter 2

1. Frank S. Mead, "Shepherd of the Senate," *Christian Herald*, November, 1948.

2. Peter Marshall, *Mr. Jones, Meet the Master*, ed. Catherine Marshall (New York: Fleming H. Revell Co., a division of Baker Publishing House, 1950), 135–136. Used by permission of Baker Publishing Group.

3. Charles Wesley, "And Can It Be That I Should Gain?"

4. Wesley, "And Can It Be That I Should Gain?"

5. Billy Graham, *How to Be Born Again* (Waco, Tex.: Word Books, 1977), 118–121. Used by permission of W Publishing, a division of Thomas Nelson, Inc., Nashville, Tennessee. All rights reserved.

6. Peter Marshall, *Mr. Jones, Meet the Master*, ed. Catherine Marshall (New York: Fleming H. Revell Co., a division of Baker Publishing House, 1950), 135–136. Used by permission of Baker Publishing Group.

Chapter 3

1. Brian McCollum, "Eminem on Top: 2002 Brought Giant Success, Steely Focus," *Detroit Free Press*, December 28, 2002, http://72.14.203.104/search/q=cache:lmjzEbCFZ-0J:www.freep.com/entertainment/newsandreviews/em28_20021228.htm, accessed December 20, 2005.

Chapter 4

1. Earl D. Radmacher, "Salvation: A Necessary Work of God," in Understanding Christian Theology, ed. Charles R. Swindoll and Roy B. Zuck (Nashville: Thomas Nelson, 2003), 846.

2. Radmacher, "Salvation," 847–852.

Contact Information

Harvest Ministries
Post Office Box 4000
Riverside, California 92514-4000
1-800-821-3300
www.harvest.org

Insight for Living
Post Office Box 269000
Plano, Texas 75026-9000
1-800-772-8888
www.insight.org